Wrestling with God

Commentary on the Book of Jonah

Daniel Arnold

Published in French in 2004 :
Jonas. Bras de fer avec un Dieu de grâce
Editions Emmaüs, route de Fenil 40, CH-1806 Saint-Légier, Switzerland

English translation: Henriette L. Ludwig

All Scripture quotations are taken from the NASB unless otherwise stated.

ABREVIATIONS

ANET	Old Near Eastern Texts relating to the Old Testament, J.B. PRITCHARD
BA	Bible Annotée, Frédéric GODET
CBQ	Catholic Biblical Quarterly
Col	Bible à la Colombe
Dar	Bible Darby
FC	Bible en Français Courant
JETS	Journal of the Evangelical Theological Society
JBL	Journal of Biblical Literature
Jér	Bible de Jérusalem
JSOT	Journal for the Study of the Old Testament
KJ	King James
LXX	Greek Septuagint Version
NASB	New American Standard Bible
NBC	New Bible Commentary D.W.B. ROBINSON
NDB	Nouveau Dictionnaire Biblique
NEB	New English Bible
NEG	Bible nouvelle édition de Genève
NIV	New International Version
Seg	Bible Segond
Sem	Bible du Semeur
TOB	Traduction œcuménique de la Bible
TWOT	Theological Wordbook of the Old Testament
ZAW	Zeitschrift für alttestamentliche Wissenschaft

TABLE OF CONTENTS

COMMENTARY

PREFACE

Jonah is a fascinating book. It takes only ten minutes to read, but ten years of study cannot explain all of the questions it raises. Jonah is a book which can be read hundreds of times. Whenever we read it again, we are caught up in a thrilling reflection of ourselves and of God, without ever tiring of it. Reading Jonah piques our curiosity, stimulates our imagination, and strikes the sensitive chords of our innermost selves. Jonah makes us laugh, smile, reflect, meditate, discuss, share, pray, confess. Sometimes we are even turned around and transformed.

Jonah is a book which is easily accessible and open to every public: to children, theology students, or simple laymen in search of a stimulating book. Jonah is a choice morsel for a preacher, a Sunday school teacher, the moderator of a discussion group. Each of them is assured of his listeners' interest, who will not fail to expand the account in their imagination. Some consider this story to be the best missionary tract of the Bible; others view it as a biting satire of God's people, or a book of psychoanalytical introspection, or even a doctrinal teaching on God's character.

Yet how should we tackle the study of such a comprehensive book? This commentary proposes two means of access. The first part, entitled "Introduction", is meant for readers who already have thorough knowledge of Jonah's story, having already read and meditated on it in the past. The second part, entitled "Commentary", is a better starting point for beginners who are reading Jonah for the first time. However, both parts complement each other. Some references serve as passageways between the two, and allow those who wish to do so to deal in depth with a specific point. The *Introduction* emphasizes the book's literary characteristics and focuses on the dominant traits of the story's characters. It evaluates the questions linked to historicity. The chapter on intertextuality lets the reader go beyond the story and position himself within the framework of the great divine revelation given to mankind. The *Commentary* follows and explains the text, verse by verse, and tries to shed light on both God's and Jonah's courses of action. It also explains the conflict-laden relationship between God and his prophet.

PART I

INTRODUCTION

LITERARY CHARACTERISTICS

A Fascinating Book

There are many different eulogies on Jonah's story. "The book of Jonah is one of the easiest and most interesting books to read in the Bible. One author says it is the most beautiful story ever written in so small a compass"[1] "The episodes link together unexpectedly, using extraordinarily lean storytelling: no descriptions, very terse dialogues, fast-paced action." says another[2]. One theologian feels that despite the brevity of the text, "no prophet's name is better known by the man on the street."[3] Another states that "Jonah is the only bit of humour in the Old Testament."[4] C.H. Cornill's testimony is no doubt the most poignant: "I have read the Book of Jonah at least a hundred times, and I will publicly avow that I cannot even now take up this marvellous book, nay, nor even speak of it, without the tears rising to my eyes, and my heart beating higher. This apparently trivial book is one of the deepest and grandest that was ever written, and I should like to say to everyone who approaches it, 'Take off thy shoes, for the place whereon thou standest is holy ground'"[5]

The account's simplicity, conciseness, dynamics, depth and sense of imagination should be particularly emphasized amongst its many other qualities.

---

1 Jensen p. 23.

2 Mora, *Jonah un conte théologique*, p. 38.

3 Elias Bickerman quoted by Lacocque p. 34.

4 Loretz quoted by Robert North p. 133.

5 *The Prophets of Israel,* p. 170, quoted by Gaebelein, *Four Minor Prophets*, p. 58.

A Concise and Simple Account

Jonah's story is only 48 verses long. In the Old Testament, only the books of Obadiah and Haggai are shorter than Jonah, and the scroll of Nahum is of equivalent length.[6] The book of Jonah could be printed on half a page of a modern-day daily newspaper. As one author emphasizes: "The book of Jonah has the advantage of being brief and written in a compact style, bubbling with life. It is an invitation to read it through at one sitting, even to read it several times."[7]

The account is not only concise, but easy to follow. The framework is simple: God asks Jonah to proclaim a message to the Ninevites. The number of characters in the account is restricted to a minimum: God, Jonah and two groups of pagans (the sailors and the Ninevites). The characteristics of individuals are clearly defined, even closely trimmed, because everything is in black and white, but in an inverted fashion. The pagans, who start off with a bad reputation (aren't the Ninevites murderers, 1:2, and the sailors idol-worshipers, 1:5?), behave like model citizens, whereas Jonah–the prophet of God and "son of truth"–remains fundamentally rebellious against God throughout the story.

The author omits some information which would divert the reader's attention and make the story unnecessarily long. Thus, he does not specify what kind of fish swallows Jonah, but simply says it is "great". Nothing is said about the dangers of the voyage to Nineveh, nor of the violent reactions that Jonah's preaching might have provoked amongst this bloodthirsty people. The Ninevites' conversion is not rationally explained, which several commentators attempt to do when defending the account's historicity. Jonah's reaction to God's last words is also omitted, leaving the reader with two questions.[8]

---

6 Taking into account the number of words. Obadiah represents 50% of Jonah and 90% of Haggai.

7 Bauer, p. 11

8 There is the question which God addresses to his prophet and the question which the reader asks himself about Jonah's reply.

… and Intriguing

…uld not be equated with
…is actually extremely dense
…unique, but it is constantly

…thing the opposite way. His
… frenzied activity and
… he is a prophet, he refuses
…ning quietly where he is in
…d, in the opposite direction
…eeks and finds a ship, then
…ssage was commonly paid
…03). Then suddenly, in the
…ophet sinks into complete
…ew in its efforts to keep the
…e hold and falls into a deep
…m out of his lethargy, he
…estions, but offers no help
…s God when asked to do so
…" 1:6), but he cares enough
…way out of their precarious
…*ow me into the sea,' he*
…'" (1:12). It is something
…n't lift a foot to carry it out.
…ard.
…ences another twist. Jonah
… towards God. The prophet
… which he expresses his
…ds the Almighty. Jonah's
… that many commentators
… to be a foreign object.
…s been swallowed by a fish
have such a positive outlook on life? Jonah's optimism seems out of place. On the ship, where there is some hope of survival from the human point of view, the prophet seems to be resigned to death, whereas in the fish, with death

apparently imminent, he expresses himself as if he has been saved.

In Chapter 3 we have yet another change of scene. Jonah finally undertakes the voyage he had refused in Chapter 1, but contrary to the trip to Tarshish, the voyage to Nineveh runs smoothly, and is dealt with in one sentence (3:3). The same conciseness and absence of difficulties mark the prophet's activities in the Assyrian metropolis: he only preaches for one day, with one phrase, in one single verse, with an unprecedented result.

In Chapter 4, Jonah surprises us again. He responds to the success of his mission with bitterness. He refuses to leave the city he didn't want to go to, and three times he asks to die (4:3, 8, 9), despite the fact that his mission has been accomplished.

The diversity of the prophet's behaviour is intriguing and enlivens the account. The "adventures of Jonah" make for exciting reading.

The account's dynamic aspect is reinforced by the pagans' frenzied activity whenever they are driven by despair. The sailors pray to their gods, throw the cargo overboard, call Jonah to action, row towards the shore with all their strength, call upon God whilst trembling with fear, whereas the Ninevites, and particularly their king, push repentance to the limit, and almost to the absurd, by forcing even their domestic animals to fast and wear the trappings of mourning.

As we turn to God, we see that he is omnipresent in the account: he commands Jonah to carry out a mission, makes the wind blow, sends a fish to swallow the prophet, then orders the fish to release him. In Chapter 3, God repeats his command of the mission to Jonah, then in Chapter 4 he twice asks him about his irritation. He also makes a vine[9] grow which he then destroys with a worm. He lets an east wind blow, and the account ends with God's longest statement, which explains to Jonah the reasons why he insists on saving the Ninevites.

---

[9] See footnote 16 p. 138 for the identification of this plant.

God is active, but his actions are often puzzling. Why save the Ninevites? This is a unique situation under the old covenant. Why insist so adamantly for Jonah to accomplish the mission, rather than choosing a different, less recalcitrant prophet? Why threaten Jonah's life and that of an entire ship's crew to save a sinful city? How can God's goodness be expressed by such an act? Isn't there a contradiction between the goal pursued, i.e. the offer of pardon proposed to the Ninevites, and the methods used: the threat of destroying a rebellious prophet and an apparently innocent crew?

The book of Jonah is captivating. The framework is simple, yet at the same time complex. The account is both concise and rich, dynamic and profound.[10]

The Surrealism of Certain Events

The book of Jonah is complex, not only because of its characters' atypical behaviour, but also because of the miracles mentioned.

1. Jonah is swallowed by a sea monster which does not devour him, but instead saves him from drowning.
2. The "three days and three nights" in the fish's belly do not trouble the prophet, because he composes a poem of gratitude.
3. The complete, immediate and profound repentance of an entire bloodthirsty people is the result of the minimalistic preaching of a reluctant prophet.
4. The growth of a tree is miraculously accelerated with the sole purpose of giving shade to a man who is already protected by a shelter.

---

10 "This account may appear slim, but it packs an explosive theological charge." (Mora, *Jonah un conte théologique*, p. 38). "The apparent simplicity of Jonah's story is deceiving; and even a superficial analysis raises a number of thorny questions." (Scherman p. xxi). "There is probably no other book of the Old Testament which presents so many riddles which are so difficult to solve than those in the book of Jonah" (*BA* p. 116). "Jonah must be read with the awareness that the problems it poses are theological, philosophical, psychological and political" (Lacocque p. 76).

The exceptional dimension of these events is reinforced by the use of the word "great" (*gadôl*) fourteen times (twice 7, the perfect number).[11] Eight realities are considered to be "great": the *city* of Nineveh (1:2; 3:2, 3; 4:11), the *wind* on the sea (1:4), the *storm* (1:4, 12), the *fish* (1:17), the sailors' *fear* (1:10, 16), the *nobles* of the city (3:5, 7), Jonah's *displeasure* (4:1) and his *joy* (4:6).[12] These terms are put in pairs or groups of four:

- Nineveh, the city of men, is described by this word four times.
- The elements linked to the sea are mentioned four times in connection with this term (the tempest twice, the wind once and the fish once).
- This term is used for the pagans four times (twice for the sailors and twice for the nobles of Nineveh).
- Jonah's mood is intensified twice by this adjective (irritation and joy).

The surrealism of all of these events and the circumstances which surround them fascinates our imagination, stimulates our curiosity, leads our intelligence astray. Are we looking at a tall tale or a story from *Arabian Nights*? Or on the contrary, are we dealing with an historical account which describes the extraordinary, mysterious and disconcerting interventions of the creator God who reveals himself to his creatures in a completely new manner?

---

[11] This represents one third of the number of times the word *gadôl* is used in the minor prophets. For a general study of the vocabulary in Jonah see: Baruch Halpern and Richard Elliott Friedman ("Composition and Paronomasia in the Book of Jonah" in *Hebrew Annual Review* 4 [1980] p. 79-92); F. Derek Kidner ("The Distribution of Divine Names in Jonah" in *Tyndale Bulletin* 21 [1970] p. 126-128) and Raymond B. Dillard (p. 393).

[12] Translators have unfortunately not always translated *gadôl* with the adjective "great".

The Atypical Character of Events and Persons

The book of Jonah often presents aspects which are diametrically opposed to those presented in other Biblical texts or to those encountered in daily life.

1. Jonah is the only "missionary" prophet (see Commentary 1:1-2 on p. 100).
2. He is the only prophet who goes to the west of Israel, and into the Mediterranean.
3. He is the only prophet who rebels against God and lives to tell the tale. The book of 1–2 Kings reports the case of the two disobedient prophets whom God punished by death (1 Kings 13:1-32; 20:35-36). Of course, men of God such as Moses, Gideon and Jeremiah asked God questions when they were called, but they obediently carried out their ministry afterwards. Jonah, however, doesn't ask any questions. Instead, he begins by disobeying God before carrying out his task.
4. The book of Jonah is the only canonical writing in the form of a narrative genre amongst the minor prophets. It consists not of oracles but of stories (Chapters 1, 3 and 4), and poetry (Chapter 2). The sole prophetic utterance is only five words long in Hebrew *("Forty more days and Nineveh will be overturned."* 3:4).
5. Jonah does not shy away from his mission out of fear that the pagans will oppose him and kill him, but rather because he is afraid that the pagans will listen to him and actually repent.
6. For Jonah, the danger comes not from the "bad guys", the Ninevites, but from a compassionate God who sends a storm to sink the ship which is transporting the rebellious prophet.
7. The fish, who is the size of a veritable sea monster, does not devour Jonah, but instead saves him and moves him to joy and praise, whereas an apparently harmless worm drives Jonah to suicidal despair.

A Book for Reflection

The author has taken pains to write a book which stimulates reflection. In order to do so, he sometimes holds back certain information for a time. The most obvious example is that of Jonah's disobedience: the prophet's refusal is presented at the beginning of the book (1:3), but *the reason* for his behaviour is not stated until the last chapter, after he has carried out his mission (4:2). Another example is linked to the deeper meaning of the divine mission, which is not revealed until the very last verse of the book (4:11).

Sometimes the narrator even sends the reader on a wild goose chase, just like many novelists do today.[13] Thus, by revealing only the Ninevites' evil side at the start of the account (1:2), then the imminent destruction of Nineveh in Chapter 3 (3:4), the narrator suggests during three fourths of his story that God wished to destroy the city, although the entire "operation Nineveh" was meant to save it from destruction.

The explanations provided by Jonah to the sailors about the reasons for his voyage (probably when he boarded ship: *"They knew he was running away from the LORD, because he had already told them so."* 1:10) are not immediately communicated to the reader. In the same way, Jonah's intercession for his salvation takes place at the bottom of the sea, when the prophet is engulfed by the waters, but is not recounted until after the fish has intervened (2:2, 7).

---

[13] "Jonah is a 'strange' book of the Bible," according to E. Bickerman. Strange because the reader is deliberately put in an uncomfortable situation. It piques his curiosity, he feels challenged to unmask the author's true intentions ." (Lacocque p. 61). There are very many questions. Landes (*Textual 'Information Gaps'...* p. 274): "I have noted no fewer than 63 places in the text where the author's deliberate or inadvertent withholding of information poses at least some interpretive issue for the reader and, in addition, 13 places where narrative features create a dissonance in the logic or coherence of the story." According to Person p. 73, in 1:8-9, the sailors ask Jonah four questions, but he replies only to the last one.

Reflection is also encouraged by the fact that the author does not answer all of the important questions raised by the account. We are not referring to the questions about the type of fish or the particular circumstances which might have pushed the Ninevites to repent (the kingdom's weakness, political instability, military threat, natural catastrophe, solar eclipse), because these questions, which are debated by commentators (see p. 139), remain secondary. The questions which are important for the account's comprehension and which remain unanswered deal with the divine mission and the prophet's behaviour. Why does God ask Jonah to carry out this ministry which is so atypical of the Old Testament? Why does the rebellious prophet flee abroad instead of simply staying in his country? How can Jonah's passivity on the ship be explained? Why doesn't God let Jonah peacefully camp at the edge of Nineveh after carrying out his mission? Why is God prepared to let men die (Jonah and the sailors) to save sinners of the worst kind? Why does God use exceptional methods (miracles of the fish and the vine) to intervene in Jonah's life? (God could have saved Jonah from drowning by letting him be fished out of the water by the sailors.)

The author also stimulates reflection with questions *in the account* for which no answers are provided. For example, the captain asks Jonah *"How can you sleep?"* Later on, the sailors ask the prophet about his flight: *"What do you do?"* In both cases, Jonah does not answer the sailors. These pertinent questions are also asked by many readers. By posing these questions, the narrator encourages *all* of his readers to ask them. Another example is found at the end of the book. The last verse is a question which God asks Jonah. Because no answer is provided, the reader is encouraged to reply to God's question himself.[14]

---

[14] The "reflective" nature of the book of Jonah has led to very different interpretations. *Cahiers Évangile. Supplément 110* presents a wide range of interpretations: rabbinic (Sr Anne-Catherine Avril), patristic (Lucile Villey), Islamic (Jean-Louis Déclais), medieval (Gilbert Dahan), Voltairean (Danièle Sion) and modern (Frédéric Boyer).

A Pleasant but Serious Book

The account presents dramatic situations: a city is about to be annihilated, a ship is about to sink, a disobedient prophet exposes himself to his God's wrath. Nevertheless, the account does not cause any nightmares and is perfectly suitable for a younger audience, as no-one dies in the story and all dangers are averted. Furthermore, the narration is pleasant. Jonah's serene calm during the storm (he is sleeping soundly) and in the fish (he praises his LORD, confident that he will soon be freed) evokes a peaceful atmosphere. The danger is there, but the prophet never panics, because he is confident of God's goodness. The only moment of anguish the prophet has is linked to his drowning, but his distress is reported in Chapter 2, when the reader has already been informed that the prophet has been saved.[15]

A number of commentators who generally have a critical approach to the text point out the account's comic tone, and speak of Jonah ironically and sarcastically. They see the narrator mocking the prophet's puerile, childish and exaggerated reactions. To them, Jonah represents a nationalistic Jewish fringe group who was insensitive to God's love for the pagans. The reader would thus be prompted to laugh at the prophet. This approach to the text can only be considered if the account of Jonah were to be accepted as literary fiction.

Before embarking on a detailed discussion of the question and a refutation of this approach (see p. 75-94), we can already note that the book presents itself as being historical, and that the Jewish people, Jesus and the apostles (Mt 12:39-41; 16:4; Lk 11:29-32), as well as the church during the greater part of its history never doubted the historicity of the events. Thus, this historicity makes an ironic reading highly improbable. No-one laughs in the account itself: the sailors

15 In contrast, one could say that some of the apocalyptic visions of other prophetic books might arouse the reader's fear. For example, the visions of hybrid and ferocious animals in Daniel 7 and 8, sources of evil and oppression, are terrifying, and Daniel himself was physically affected by them (Da 7:28; 8:27).

fight for their lives; the Ninevites wear mourning and fast; Jonah rants against God, and God does the same to his prophet. The mood is not joyful[16] except for Jonah, just for a day (4:6). On the other hand, serenity is present throughout, both from God (who controls the events), and in Jonah (who has confidence in the divine patience and mercy towards himself).

The book of Jonah provides the account of a dramatic situation which ends well, thanks to God's mercy and the common sense of men who finally recognize their wrongs. The book's "goody-two shoes" tone does not result from mockery and ridicule, but from joy and relief after a series of catastrophes which have been barely avoided. The narrator convincingly communicates that God is good and compassionate, slow to anger and rich in goodness. Although the tone is pleasant, it remains serious, because the reasons which have led to the dramatic events remain latently inherent in the lives of many men.

It is nevertheless possible to smile at Jonah's stubbornness whilst still holding fast to the account's historicity. The irony comes from Jonah's pen (see p. 95) which criticizes his past obstinacy against the divine plan.

---

16 Feinberg "The Jews read this book during the solemn hours of the Day of Atonement" p. 133.

THE CHARACTERS

To understand the book of Jonah, we must first analyse its main characters, because Jonah, God, the sailors and the Ninevites all exhibit extraordinary behaviour. We begin our study with Jonah, as he has the most complex personality. He moves from one extreme to the other: from passiveness to activity, from suicidal irritation to overflowing joy, from disobedience to obedience, from flight to the west to refusal to leave his safe shelter east of Nineveh.

Secondly, we will look at God, who also seems to present different facets of himself. He wants to judge the Ninevites, but not without giving them one last chance to repent and be saved. God confides to Jonah the task of warning them, but is so set on the completion of this mission of grace to the Ninevites that he is prepared to kill his prophet if the latter does not obey. The conflict-laden relationship between Jonah and the LORD lies at the heart of the entire account.

Thirdly, we will analyse the pagans' behaviour. Despite the fact that the sailors' and the Ninevites' behaviour is not typical of the common behaviour of pagans, it can be more easily analysed, as it shows one particular facet throughout the entire book. Contrary to the *ever-changing* portrait of the prophet and the *progressive* revelation of the LORD, the sailors' and the Ninevites' behaviour throughout the account is *stable and uniform* from start to finish. The sailors and the Ninevites form two groups which are so well-characterized and which are so similar that it is possible to view the navigators of the west and the citizens of the east in the same way.

Jonah

Jonah is such a complex personality that views about him will invariably differ from one commentator to the other. (1)

Some see in him a type of carnal man, and the entire account as deriding the prophet. (2) Others consider Jonah to be a courageous prophet who is basically attached to his people, for whom he sacrifices himself at the risk of exposing himself to divine judgment. (3) A third group, torn between the prophet's faults and his qualities, is inclined to consider him as schizophrenic personality who oscillates between the best and the worst traits. (4) It is also possible to see Jonah as a man of God who is deeply attached to the LORD for the basic essentials, but who disagrees with him on a particular point. We feel that this last approach best explains Jonah's contrasting behaviour.

1. The Worst Kind of Prophet

Jonah is often described in very negative terms. He is "mulish, sinister, petty, ludicrous, good-for-nothing, disobedient and hypocritical, remarkably difficult to understand why God bothers about him… narrow, chauvinistic"[1] or "petty, narrow-minded and obstinate"[2]. He is a man "whose theology was as clear as ice – and twice as cold."[3] Thus, "The greatness and the goodness of God are enhanced against the background of Jonah's meanness and malevolence."[4] In short, Jonah is "a religious psychological monster".[5]

Some commentators divest the prophet of all positive characteristics: "The writer has progressively and deliberately destroyed Jonah's credibility, making him one who strikes out too readily at the world when it does not suit him."[6] "The general argument that some parts of the portrait are not unsympathetic is simply inadequate."[7]

---

1 Sherwood "Cross-Currents in the Book of Jonah" p. 53, 60.
2 Lacocque p. 35.
3 Kohlenberger p. 21, who quotes one of his former professors.
4 Allen p. 194.
5 G. von Rad quoted by par Lacocque p. 35.
6 Hauser p. 37.
7 Payne, "Jonah from the Perspective of Its Audience", p. 266.

2. A Martyr for Israel

Other commentators take a more positive view of Jonah. Of course, they recognize that Jonah often appears to be suicidal. In the midst of the furious storm, he descends into the hold and falls into deep slumber, perhaps hoping to sink with the ship, instead of helping the sailors keep the ship afloat (1:5); when the storm whips up, he proposes that the sailors throw him overboard (1:12); at the end of his mission, he twice asks the LORD to take his life (4:3, 8). This suicidal attitude can, however, be explained in a positive way if Jonah is seen as a martyr for Israel. The prophet could be saying to himself that if he does not go to Nineveh, its inhabitants would not hear God's threat. Consequently, they would not repent, being ignorant of any imminent danger, which would unavoidably lead to the city's destruction. If Nineveh were destroyed, the Assyrians would have to renounce their imperialistic ambitions...and the kingdom of Israel would be saved. Jonah would thus accept destroying himself to make God's plan fail. Jewish tradition defends this point of view (see footnote 10, p. 105).

3. A Schizophrenic Personality

The explanation of "Jonah's martyrdom" does not, however, explain his suicide wish after having carried out his mission. That is why other commentators, without bypassing certain positive aspects of the prophet–particularly his courage and righteousness–end with Jonah's fluctuating nature, which goes from one extreme to the other: feverish, then static; mute, then talkative; rebellious, then thankful; depressive, then euphoric. Above all, the prophet appears to be a schizophrenic personality who is difficult, and even impossible, to understand and who slips between our fingers like a fish.

4. A Man with a Remarkable Character

A fourth approach emphasizes many of Jonah's qualities. Prior to dealing with them in detail, two remarks are necessary. The first concerns the nature of the mission confided to Jonah. Have all of the prophet-bashers taken into account the difficulty of his mission? To travel over a thousand kilometres from home to a bloodthirsty people in order to announce God's imminent judgment to them is anything but an easy task. If you add to that the fact that the mission was not only the first but also the only one of its kind, because never before and never again did God ask a man to carry out something like that, we realize how difficult the task was and what qualities were required to carry it out successfully.[8]

The second preliminary remark is about the men whom God calls to a particular ministry. In general, God assigned such tasks to men who were pious, upright and spiritual. Of course, these men sometimes had a previous spiritual history which was somewhat tarnished (this particularly holds true for the apostle Paul, former persecutor of the church), but once they were called to the ministry, these men were dedicated to the LORD; some already had been so for a long time, some only for a short while.[9] Whether it was Abraham,

---

[8] Elijah and Elisha, two prophets who were contemporaries of Jonah, had already ministered to the pagans, but in a more limited manner (see p. 54-55). After the resurrection and ascension of Jesus Christ, the very first Christians, the majority of whom were Jewish, had difficulty accepting the *unconditional* opening of the Gospel to non-Jews. Despite all of Christ's teaching, Peter had to receive a threefold vision at Jaffa (the port where Jonah embarked! Acts 10:9-16) to understand that *"God does not show favoritism but accepts men from every nation who fear him and do what is right."* (Acts 10:34-35 NIV). Paul often encountered opposition from the Judaizers on the subject of full integration of non-Jews into the church. The goal of the conference of Jerusalem, a sort of first Christian council, was to regulate the question of the acceptance of Gentiles into the church (Acts 15:1-29). These examples show the difficulty which the believers who were attached to the LORD had with entering into a whole new phase of God's plan. Jonah's mission was a world preview of universal opening with the grace shown to the non-Jews.

[9] This remark can certainly not be applied to the men who inherited their ministry from their father (as was the case of the Levites, high priests and kings).

Moses, David, Old Testament prophets or apostles—all were above the norm. They were spiritual models of their times.[10]

Regarding the ministry to the Ninevites, would it not be reasonable to think that God would have confided such a delicate mission to a man with proven spiritual qualities, perhaps the best of his generation? In any case, Jonah has many obvious qualities.

Courage. Jonah is courageous at every test. He accepts voyages on land and by sea, not for pleasure, but by conviction or obligation. There were many dangers involved: storms and pirates at sea, discomfort and brigands on land. After the exile, Ezra points out the dangers which lie in store for travellers who journeyed from Mesopotamia to Palestine (Ezra 8:21-23, 31). It comes as no surprise that the Hebrews avoided traveling outside of the Promised Land as much as possible, because they were horrified at mixing with pagans. In spite of this, Jonah accepts two long voyages to the far ends of the known world. He lives with the sailors, faces a storm on the Mediterranean (during which he remains calm, whilst the sailors panic); he goes to Nineveh, then decides to remain near the Assyrian metropolis. He even preaches a message of condemnation to the murderous people, fearing only that he might be heard (4:2)! Jonah is even capable of composing a psalm of thanks inside a sea monster. His courage comes in part from his knowledge of God.

Knowledge of God. Jonah perfectly understands God's plans. From the very start, he knows that the goal of his mission to Nineveh is not the destruction but rather the salvation of the city (cf. 4:2). If God had wanted to destroy the city, Jonah would not have needed to inform the Ninevites of their fate.

Jonah also recognizes the gesture which sailors must carry out in order to keep their ship from sinking: they must throw their peculiar passenger into the sea (1:12). The procedure is strange, but the events prove the prophet right *("So they*

---

[10] Saul, the first king of Israel, seems to be the exception to this rule, but it must be said that God wished to give Israel a king in compliance with their carnal wish (1 Sam 8:9-22).

picked up Jonah, threw him into the sea, and the sea stopped its raging." 1:15).

Jonah can praise God when he is within the fish because he knows he is safe. The God who has begun this work of salvation will certainly carry it through to the end, and once again this is proved by the events that come to pass *("Then the LORD commanded the fish, and it vomited Jonah up onto the dry land."* 2:10). The prophet's words of praise in the fish are full of psalms and display meditation and even memorization of Scripture.

Knowledge of Scripture also makes it possible for Jonah to announce Nineveh's destiny. In less than forty days, the city is "overturned" as he had announced (see p. 137).

Finally, knowledge of God's patience and compassion (cf. 4:2) allows the prophet to argue with God. He knows that his LORD will not punish him immediately. He can sleep during the storm, because it must rage even more strongly if the ship should truly be sunk (cf. 1:13).

Some commentators think that Jonah is mistaken in thinking he can flee far from God, but Jonah never intends to escape from divine might. He is convinced that God is the LORD of the earth and the sea. The only motive for his flight is his disagreement with God's plan (see p. 105).

Faith. Jonah's faith stems from his knowledge of the LORD. The prophet lives in line with what he knows about God. He can sleep during a raging tempest because he believes in God's patience and goodness. By the same token, he thanks God for saving him in the fish and before he sets foot on firm ground because he believes that the LORD will always complete the salvation he has begun. In faith Jonah announces the end of the storm to the sailors (to the point that they dissociate themselves from him). By faith he announces to the Ninevites the imminent upheaval that awaits them.

Truth. Jonah is the son *of Amittai*, that is to say the son of *truth.* When he speaks, he says the truth. He quickly reveals to the sailors that he is fleeing far from the LORD (1:10). He testifies his faith in the LORD to them (1:9) and announces how they can save themselves at the risk of his own life (*"throw me into the sea"* 1:12). Each time Jonah opens his mouth and deigns to answer the questions asked, he states the truth. The same statement holds true regarding his contact with the Ninevites. At the start of the book, he refuses to announce God's message to them, but when he finally accepts the mission, he tells them the truth, even though he doesn't like the task and there is a risk that the message could infuriate this murderous people.

Jonah is equally and fully transparent in his relationship to God. He expresses his thanks to God in the fish (2:2-7); he completes the mission he has promised to carry out while he was still in the fish's stomach (2:11); he voices his irritation after pardon has been granted to the Ninevites (4:2-3); he repeats his exasperation after the vine withers and dies (4:8-9).

Love of fellow man. Jonah is often considered to be a xenophobic nationalist who only cares about his own people's well-being.[11] Yet Jonah accepts to sacrifice his own life to save a pagan crew from a storm *("Pick me up and throw me into the sea. Then the sea will become calm for you."* 1:12). He is also willing to risk his life to offer the Ninevites the message of salvation. Of course, he only does so after much hesitation, and, it seems, with great reluctance (cf. 4:2), but he does it nonetheless. Thus, "Biblical" love is characterised more by acts than by sentiment.

However, brotherly love is a field where Jonah has yet to make some progress, because despite the reality of his love, it is not yet on the level of the love which God has for all mankind. In fact, the book of Jonah is basically an instruction book on God's love of man.

---

[11] This opinion is partly inspired by 2 Kings 14:25, which indicates that Jonah prophesied that Israel would re-establish a border to the east of its kingdom. It should be noted that Jonah's words about the re-establishment of a border at the time of Jeroboam II was a *prophecy*, i.e. a word of God and not the opinion of a man who was exhorting his king to start a war against his neighbors. Furthermore, the author of Kings indicates that Israel suffered greatly at the hands of the Syrians (2 Kings 14:26). The recovery of the border is thus presented as a war of liberation which puts an end to *"how bitterly everyone in Israel, whether slave or free, was suffering"*, as Israel had lost all of its allies *("there was no one to help them" NIV)*.

Jonah may be criticized about his restrictive love, but how many men do better than he? Who is prepared to give his love and pardon to the most perverse beings if they repent? Who is prepared to pardon in the way God pardons? Jonah is at least frank. He expresses his opposition to God.

Perseverance. Let us note one last characteristic of Jonah: perseverance. The prophet carries out his commitments to the hilt. He may be reticent about obeying God's orders, but once he has given his word *("What I have vowed I will make good. "* 2:9 NIV), he carries it out immediately, even if it greatly displeases him.

Jonah's obstinacy manifests itself especially in his resistance of God's plan to save the Ninevites. Thus, Jonah goes to the other end of the world to express his disagreement with the LORD (see Commentary, p. 105). He sleeps during a raging storm to show God that he refuses to listen to him (see p. 109). He prefers to be thrown into the sea than to repent. Finally, it is only in the most extreme situation, at the bottom of the sea, that he bends his knee before God (see p. 122). But after carrying out his mission, he rears up again and vociferously expresses his disagreement (4:2). He sticks to his opinion and refuses to leave Nineveh, because he wants to have the last word. He pays with his person by remaining on the fringe of Nineveh in the same manner in which he had paid with his person and his money when he left for Tarshish (1:3), He makes the effort to build a little hut which he then refuses to leave, despite the extreme climatic conditions (4:8). In the same vein, in his final dialogue with God, he refuses to reconsider and sticks to his guns: *"Then God said to Jonah, 'Do you have good reason to be angry about the plant?' And he said, 'I have good reason to be angry, even to death.'"* (4:9).

Jonah is obviously stubborn. Is this an asset or a flaw? It all depends on what side of the coin you're looking at. Nevertheless, we can generally say that perseverance is an asset. It characterizes a man who has convictions and is not stopped either by unfavourable circumstances or other people's opposition. The success of great projects throughout the course of history is generally due to perseverance, the tenacity of those who swim upstream to see their plans through. Thus, if Jonah ends up failing in his opposition to God's plan, it is simply because he finds himself face to face with someone who is more determined than he is. The test of will with God as his opponent turns to the latter's advantage, because above all, God wants Jonah's mission to be successful. The LORD's resolve is stronger than Jonah's.

Jonah has a number of moral and spiritual qualities, but he still rebels against God. The meaning of his rebellion and his flight to Tarshish shall be examined in the Commentary, because the test of strength between the LORD and his prophet constitutes the framework of the entire book.

God

In the book of Jonah, God reveals two very different aspects of his character. First, he shows himself as the judging God; then, progressively, the element of grace becomes increasingly apparent.

Divine Wrath

The start of the book is characterized by God's displeasure with sinful men. The LORD takes radical measures against the Ninevites, because their *"wickedness has come up"* before him (1:2). He then lets a furious wind blow across the sea because of Jonah's disobedience (1:4). The sailors are also stricken by divine wrath, because they have taken in the rebellious prophet in full knowledge of his erring ways (1:10). The storm gets worse as Jonah's obstinacy increases. He turns a blind eye to the first signs of God's anger when he goes to take nap in the hold (1:5). The storm is also the result of the sailors' refusal to disavow the wrongdoer (they try to reach the shore instead of throwing Jonah into the sea 1:13).

Later on, God's judgment becomes shadowy. When God repeats his call to Jonah to go to Nineveh, he no longer speaks of the Ninevites' *"evil ways"*, but simply of a *"proclamation"* to be announced (3:2). Jonah predicts that the city will soon be overturned (3:4). However, his message does not necessarily imply destruction, but possibly also a repentance (see p. 137). Faced with Jonah's discontent after the Ninevites' change of behaviour, God gives his prophet a reminder, not with the threat of death by storm but by making him uncomfortable with blazing sunshine.

God's Grace

God's grace is presented at the beginning, but in a very discreet manner. From the start, Jonah's mission is conceived as a matter of grace and that is how Jonah understands it (4:2), but the reader is not informed of this intention until the last chapter. Before destroying Nineveh like Sodom and Gomorrah had been destroyed in the past, God wants to warn the Ninevites to give them a final occasion to repent.

God gets angry at Jonah (and with the sailors who have taken him in), but his judgment is progressive so as to give the prophet and the sailors time to repent. The minute repentance has taken place, God ceases the danger *("and the sea stopped its raging"* as soon as Jonah is thrown into the water) or sends an unexpected rescuer *("the LORD appointed a great fish to swallow Jonah"* 1:17).

At first, Jonah is saved from death, but he remains sequestered within the fish for several days *"Jonah was inside the stomach of the fish three days and three nights"* 1:17), possibly to bring him to the shore, but perhaps also to convince him to carry out his mission. In fact, the narrator indicates that Jonah will be freed just after having signalled the prophet's intention to carry out his vow (2:9b-10).

God's grace comes to light when the LORD reverses his decision to destroy Nineveh after all of its citizens repent (*"then God relented concerning the calamity which He had declared He would bring upon them. And He did not do it."* 3:10).

God's grace towards Jonah also manifests itself in Chapter 4. God even undertakes different efforts to release the prophet from his predicament and to convince him that God's action is sound.

In a general way, God's divine grace is conveyed by his patience with sinners and the pardon which he grants when they repent.

God's Astonishing Actions

God is so intent on completing his mission to the Ninevites–making sure they have one last chance to be saved–that he uses exceptional means to make it work.[12] All of creation participates: the winds on the sea in the west (1:4) and over the land in the east (4:8); creatures great (1:17; 2:10) and small (4:7); plants (4:6). All of the elements of creation obey immediately. The only one who has trouble with submission is Jonah. But Jonah is not just anyone–he is a prophet of God with obvious moral and spiritual qualities.

God insists on carrying out his plan by means of Jonah, despite his reticence. God does not choose another prophet, nor does he consider using non-human means (the Creator God could have written a message in the sky for the Ninevites, just like he could have revealed himself through dreams and visions). Yet God chooses Jonah to see his plan through.

God is prepared to do anything to carry out his plan, even to let Jonah perish if he continues to refuse, even to drown an entire ship's crew who supports the prophet. This is the second source of astonishment in this book. How can *"a gracious and compassionate God, slow to anger and abundant in loving-kindness"* (4:2) go so far as to sacrifice

---

12 Some commentators are very critical of God: Serge Frolov ("Returning the Ticket: God and his Prophet in the Book of Jonah" in *JSOT* 86, 1999, p. 92-95) and Phyllis Trible ("A Tempest in a Text: Ecological Soundings in the Book of Jonah" in *Theology Digest* 43, 1996, 303-312). Regarding the storm sent by God, Trible (p. 303, 305) says: "Yahweh pursues Jonah. The pursuit comes not in measured response but in violent extravagance… A single divine act has terrified the entire world that Jonah inhabits." (p. 303). On Chapters 1 and 2: "Yahweh… exercises crushing power. Bending nature to the divine will, the deity stalks disobedient Jonah and in that pursuit endangers the lives of innocent sailors" (p. 305). Trible revolts against the "major dissonances" in the account (p. 311).

his own prophet to carry out his work of salvation? Isn't it a contradiction to want to save atrocious sinners and to kill a faithful believer with many spiritual and moral attributes?

The exceptional methods which the LORD applies testify to his determination to accomplish a *prophetic* sign which shows the extent of his grace.

God's Wish to Instruct

The book of Jonah underscores the LORD's wish to instruct. God wants to teach the Ninevites, Jonah, Israel, the entire world.

The Ninevites. God sends Jonah to announce the divine judgment to the Ninevites, but also and primarily to give them one last chance to repent and be saved.

Jonah. Once the mission is accomplished, God does not lose interest in Jonah, but does everything to convince him of the divine plan's justness. God intervenes in creation again and miraculously makes a vine grow (4:6); he then sends a worm (4:7) and a hot wind from the east (4:8). Above all, the LORD speaks with Jonah, because in the last chapter, the majority of the words are the LORD's (approximately 70%).

The book ends with the LORD's longest verbal intervention (it contains 60% of all of the words he speaks in this book). Jonah must understand the deep meaning of God's love. God is not only the patient *judge*, *"slow to anger and abundant in loving-kindness"*, hoping for the Ninevites to repent (4:2), but he is also the *Creator* who maintains the relationship of a father to a child with the beings he has created. The pagans are immature beings "*who do not know the difference between their right and left hand*" (4:11). They are like children who are in great need of instruction.

Israel and the world. The book of Jonah is prophetic. God announces the extent of his love to Israel and, beyond his chosen people, to the entire world. The book prepares Christ's coming (see p. 67-74). The figure of God the Father emerges progressively.

The desire to instruct is so strong in the book of Jonah that it (almost) eclipses the wish to save the Ninevites. It must be said that salvation is closely linked to knowledge of God, because the announcement of grace through Jesus Christ is the way chosen by God to save the world.

> *How then will they call on Him in whom they have not believed? How will they believe in Him whom they have not heard? And how will they hear without a preacher? How will they preach unless they are sent? Just as it is written, 'How beautiful are the feet of those who bring good news! of good things...*
>
> *So faith comes from hearing, and hearing by the word of Christ. (Romans 10:14-17).*

The Pagans

The pagans' behaviour is at the same time both surprising and banal. It is surprising because it is the opposite of what a Hebrew reader would expect them to do; it is banal in the sense that it remains constant throughout the book. From start to finish in the account, the pagans do what is right and their attitude is exemplary.

When the storm grows worse, the sailors throw the freight overboad (1:5). The material loss is not a senseless gesture, but rather reflects the wisdom of people who are capable of evaluating the importance of a situation and who take the necessary measures. They add a religious effort to this gesture. To be on the safe side, they invoke *all* deities (1:5); even Jonah is urged to pray to his God (1:6). When faced with the fact that their efforts have no effect, they do not give up; they look for the cause of the problem (1:7). When Jonah is recognized as being responsible, he is not immediately lynched—he is questioned (1:8). The sailors want to know more, and they keep cool. Their concern about preventing Jonah from undergoing a severe judgment and their horror at committing murder are commendable (1:13-14). Once a solution presents itself, the sailors do not forget to thank the Creator (1:16).

The Ninevites' behaviour is even more remarkable. All of the city's inhabitants repent, without the least exception (3:5). The king takes the display of repentance to the extreme (3:7).

The contrast to the prophet is obvious. The pagans do the right thing, whereas Jonah persists in his contention of God. Of course, Jonah temporarily changes his attitude in the middle of the book (Chapters 2 and 3), but his inner attitude is not really transformed. In the long run, Jonah does not appear to change.

We note that the reader does not know what happens to the pagans afterwards. The sailors offer a sacrifice to the LORD and swear an oath when the storm is over, but nothing is mentioned about their behaviour later on. Do they become true worshipers of the LORD or do they return to their pagan beliefs? No-one knows. The Ninevites repent immediately, but no-one knows for how long. Jonah wants to wait and see, but God doesn't let him. A reader might also ask about the extent of the Ninevites' repentance. They show many exterior signs: an official fast, sackcloth and ashes, both young and old commit to it, even their animals. But are these feelings accompanied by a change of lifestyle? Of course, the king has given the order: *"But both man and beast must be covered with sackcloth; and let men call on God earnestly that each may turn from his wicked way and from the violence which is in his hands."* (3:8), but has this command been obeyed? We can hope so, without being entirely certain.[13]

Stability and Change

Stability and change are the bases of the book of Jonah. Certain characteristics of Jonah, God and the pagans evolve during the course of the account, whereas others remain constant.

The portrait of God presented by the narrator develops throughout the chapters (he goes from judgment to salvation), but God's attributes remain constant from start to finish. In fact, the goal of the mission confided to Jonah is always the Ninevites' salvation. God's repentance at the end of Chapter

---

[13] Nevertheless, it is probable that the Ninivites were sincere because God accepted their repentance. See p. 129.

3 is not merely a whim, but an attitude which could have been expected from the start, as Jonah testifies at the beginning of Chapter 4. The revelation of God is progressive, but God's attributes are unchangeable.

The portrait of Jonah also evolves during the course of the account. Yet this development is cyclical, not linear. The picture of Jonah fluctuates throughout the book: revolt and submission, silence and abundant words, irritation and joy. With God, the light gradually comes to shine, but with Jonah, fog and confusion remain. However, despite the many changes, Jonah reflects the image of a persevering and obstinate man who is set on having the last word. In conclusion, the portrait of Jonah fluctuates, but the prophet's character is constant.

The pagans are the opposite of Jonah. They remain the same from the beginning to the end. This can be seen as positive or negative. In a positive sense, the pagans always do what is right in the book of Jonah. They are like children (cf. 4:11). They are malleable and can still be taught, contrary to Israel who is hardened. In a negative sense, the pagans' behaviour is constantly changing. Their stability is rooted in their instability, with change as the only constant. We could also ask if that will be their behaviour in the future. Will the pagans continue to do what is right, or is their conduct as described in the book of Jonah characterized by its brief duration?

In conclusion, the behaviour of men–be it that of Jonah, the sailors or the Ninevites–remains enigmatic and uncertain. Some questions remain, but that is basically not a problem, because God is constant. The reader does not need to know everything about life. From the moment he recognizes God and knows he is *"a gracious and compassionate God, slow to anger and abundant in loving-kindness",* he can turn to his Creator. That is all he needs to live.

THE STRUCTURE OF THE BOOK

Two Parts

The book of Jonah has two parts: Chapters 1-2 and 3-4. One part deals with a voyage to the west across the sea; the other with a voyage to the east across land. In both cases, the destinations are at the furthest extremes of the known world at that time: Tarshish is west of the strait of Gibraltar[1] (farther than the great sea) and Nineveh lies on the northeast bank of the Tigris (farther than the second great river).[2]

The first voyage springs from disobedience and fails; the second comes from obedience and succeeds. We note that each part describes an inversion. Jonah begins by disobeying in the first part (1:3), then ends up obeying *("What I have vowed I will make good"* 2:9 NIV). In the second part, Jonah begins by obeying (3:3), then contests the LORD at the end (Chapter 4).

God always has the last word, both at the beginning and at the end. Both parts begin with the LORD's call to proclaim a message of judgment[3] to the Ninevites (1:1-2; 3:1-2) and they end with a word of grace from him. God speaks to the fish,

---

1 See footnote 5, p. 89.

2 Nineveh is on the left bank of the Tigris, i.e. east of the river. Two rivers (the Euphrates and the Tigris) had to be crossed to reach the city. Thus, in Biblical thinking, the Euphrates (the first of the the two rivers) represented the last frontier of the Promised Land (Gen 15:18; 31:21; Dt 1:7, 11:24; Jos 1:4; 1 Kings 4:21 [or 5:1]; Nh 2:7). Beyond this river, the world was dominated by the pagans and was theirs. Crossing the second river accentuated the distance from the Promised Land.

3 This is the first impression created by these words.

who releases Jonah (2:10) and he informs Jonah of his mercy towards all of the living creatures in Nineveh (4:11).[4]

A Double Linear Structure

Each part contains three sections in the following order: a preface, a stay with the pagans, a dialogue with God.

A.1	First preface	1:1-3
B.1	First stay with the pagans	1:4-16
C.1	First "dialogue" with God	1:17-2:10
A.2	Second preface	3:1-3
B.2	Second stay with the pagans	3:4-10
C.2	Second dialogue with God	4

Two Prefaces: 1:1-3 and 3:1-3

The two prefaces (A.1 and A.2) are brief. They contain the LORD's command, and use almost the same terms (two words out of three are identical: see 3:1 p. 133).

Jonah's reaction in both cases is diametrically opposed. One of God's physical characteristics ("the *face [i.e. presence]* of the LORD 1:3) and an acoustic element ("the *word* of the LORD" 3:3) are mentioned. Disobedience is marked by space: Jonah flees far from the face of the LORD, then gets bogged down in a visual, non-verbal resistance (see p. 105). On the other hand, obedience is manifested by sound: Jonah acts according to the LORD's word, then proclaims that word to the Ninevites.

---

4 A number of authors propose detailed structures: for the entire book, Duane L. Christensen ("Andrzej Panufnik and the Structure of the Book of Jonah: Icons, Music and Literary Art" p. 133-140) and Ernst R. Wendland ("Text Analysis and the Genre of Jonah [part 2]" p. 373-395); for Chapter 1: Claude Lichtert ("Par terre et par mer! Analyse rhétorique de Jonah 1") and John R. Kohlenberger ("Jonah and Nahum", p. 32 for section 1:4-16).

Two Stays among Pagans: 1:4-16 and 3:4-10

Twice Jonah stays with pagans (B.1 and B.2): a crew of sailors and the citizens of a megalopolis. The prophet has a good rapport with both groups and his influence is decisive. His words are heard and lead to salvation. The sailors end up throwing Jonah into the sea according to his advice, and by doing so they calm the storm as well as the LORD who caused it (1:15); the Ninevites repent *en masse* after Jonah preaches to them (3:4-5) and receive God's pardon (3:10). The view of both pagan groups is positive each time, because these men are receptive to God's word.

Two Dialogues with God: 1:17-2:10 and 4:1-11

The last two sections (C.1 and C.2) are characterised by an intense verbal exchange between Jonah and the LORD. It is even more obvious in view of the significant absence of communication between the prophet and his LORD in the preceding sections (B.1 and B.2).

The first verbal exchange is a monologue in which Jonah is so voluble that God can only reply by addressing…the fish (2:11)! On the other hand, the second is a perfectly balanced dialogue, because the length of speech is identical: each side speaks 47 Hebrew words. Jonah talks three times, first with a 39-word answer (4:2-3), then twice, very succinctly, with 3 and 5 words respectively (4:8, 9). The LORD also speaks three times, twice succinctly (3 and 5 words: 4:4, 9), then more abundantly at the end with 39 words (4:10-11).[5]

The words in Chapter 2 express praise, and those of Chapter 4 a lively discussion. Praise is spoken in the darkness and foul air of the fish's insides, whilst the discussion takes place under a hot sun and in the open air, abundantly wafted

[5] The LORD intervenes with his word six times in the book: five times the word is addressed to Jonah (1:1-2; 3:1-2; 4:4, 9, 10-11) and once to the fish (2:10). A seventh reference to "the word of the LORD" can be found in 3:3, when Jonah "obeyed the word of the LORD and went to Nineveh".

by a dry easterly wind. What contrasts! The physical situation is the opposite of the moral one. Jonah is delighted in the darkness, but laments in the light.[6]

Two animals are also used in these two sections. God sends a fish and a worm (1:17; 4:7). The first animal is large, good and belongs to the marine world. The second one is small, malicious and belongs to the terrestrial sphere. The fish saves Jonah from death and despair, and the worm drives the prophet into a life-threatening depression.[7]

A Concentric Structure

A second structure results from the two parts. It is concentric or chiasmic, not linear. Each part is composed of two main sections and they are introduced by a preface which functions like a sort of marshal, e.g. a section which remains on the fringe of the debates.

A.1	First preface	1:1-3
B.1	Jonah disobeys God	1:4-16
C.1	Jonah praises God	1:17-2:10
A.2	Second preface	3:1-3
C.2	Jonah obeys God	3:4-10
B.2	Jonah contests God	4

First and Last Main Structures: B.1 (1:4-16) and B.2 (4:1-11)

These two sections develop the theme of Jonah's rebellion. In Chapter 1, the prophet goes to Tarshish to flee from the LORD's view, and in Chapter 4, he is irritated by

6 We note that in Chapter 4, the only time the prophet's irritation is eased is with the *shadow* of the vine (e.g. with darkness). The prophet's joy is great (4:6).

7 One could also point out that both animals move by wiggling their body.

divine grace. In the last chapter, moreover, he begins by recalling his flight to Tarshish (4:2).[8]

In both sections, Jonah appears to wish for death. During the storm, he is passive and gives the impression of wanting to stop fighting for his life. He sleeps in the midst of the raging storm and even goes to lie at the bottom of the hold, which is a vulnerable spot (1:5; see p. 109). He apparently refuses to call on his God (1:6). Later on, he even proposes to be thrown overboard (1:12). The prophet's suicidal attitude is thus suggested several times in Chapter 1, but in Chapter 4, it is expressed in words not only twice, but three times: *"Therefore now, O LORD, please take my life from me, for death is better to me than life."* (4:3; see also 4:8, 9).

The prophet's communication with both God and men is problematic. It gives the impression of a dialogue of the deaf. In Chapter 1, Jonah launches into a non-verbal battle with the LORD which continuously intensifies. With the sailors, communication is verbal, but no less nebulous. The sailors do not understand the prophet's attitude and ask him: *"How is it that you are sleeping?"* (1:6). They ask him about his business (1:8), although he has already told them that that he is fleeing from God (1:10). They continue trying to save Jonah from death (1:13), despite the fact that he has told them that the only way to save themselves is to throw him into the sea (1:12).

In Chapter 4, the battle with God is first verbal (4:2-3), then non-verbal when Jonah decides to settle to the east of the city to see *"what would happen in the city"*. (4:5). It then becomes verbal again at the end of the chapter (4:8-9). Jonah's great joy at the apparition of the vine (4:6) is the result of a false interpretation of God's will. The repetition of the questions which God asks Jonah (*"Have you any right to be angry?"* 4:4, 9 NIV) shows that the dialogue is stagnating. The expected reply is obviously negative and yet Jonah insists on having his way: *"he became faint and begged with all his soul to die, saying, 'Death is better to me than life.'"* (4:8).

---

8 Tarshish is only mentioned twice (1:3; 4:2).

On the geographical level, Jonah is outdoors in both sections. A nasty wind is blowing: at sea, it stirs up a storm (1:4) and on land it rapidly withers the vine (4:8). On one hand, Jonah is exposed to great humidity and on the other to severe dryness (he is dehydrated and suffers from lack of protection).

In the first and last sections (B.1 and B.2), Jonah is thus both physically and spiritually on the outside (i.e. outside of God's will). We note that he is also at the antipodes of the Promised Land, because he goes to the far west on the ship (the return trip starts when Jonah is swallowed by the fish) and then east of Nineveh (a city which is located at the extreme end of Israel). In B.1, God prevents Jonah from getting to his destination and in B.2, God wants to prevent Jonah from staying where he is.

On the structural level, both sections are organised as an elaborate chiasmus (16 and 9 elements respectively: see p. 45-46). A paradox can be found at the centre of each of the structures. Jonah says he fears the LORD at the centre of B.1 [h.1] (although the entire section underscores his opposition to God's plan), then the narrator says that Jonah feels great joy at the centre of B.2 [e] (but the entire section revolves around the prophet's anger).

In the tables on the following pages (p. 45-46), the explanations (left column) have been placed parallel to the Biblical text (right column) for easier comparison.

Detailed Structure of Section B.1 (1:4-16)

a.1	Start of the storm and the sailors' fear	*4 The LORD hurled a great wind on the sea and there was a great storm on the sea so that the ship was about to break up. 5Then the sailors **became afraid***
b.1	Pagans pray to gods	*and every man cried to his god,*
c.1	Sailors' physical efforts	*and they threw the cargo which was in the ship into the sea to lighten it for them.*
d.1	Jonah is passive, but he is asked to say something	*But Jonah had gone below into the hold of the ship, lain down and fallen sound asleep. 6So the captain approached him and said, "How is it that you are sleeping? Get up, call on your god Perhaps your god will be concerned about us so that we will not perish."*
e.1	The sailors ask themselves what they should do	*7 Each man said to his mate, "Come, let us cast lots so we may learn on whose account this calamity has struck us."*
f.1	Jonah is found guilty	*So they cast lots and the lot fell on Jonah.*
g.1	The sailors ask Jonah about his sin	*Then they said to him, "Tell us, now! On whose account has this calamity struck us? What is your occupation? And where do you come from? What is your country? From what people are you?"*
h.1	Jonah confesses that he fears the LORD	*9 He said to them, "I am a Hebrew, and I **fear** the LORD, the God of heaven, who made the sea and the dry land."*
h.2	The sailors are terrified	*10 **Then the men became extremely frightened***
g.2	The sailors ask Jonah about his sin	*and they said to him, "How could you do this?"*
f.2	Jonah has already confessed his sin	*(For the men knew that he was fleeing from the presence of the LORD, because he had told them.)*
e.2	The sailors ask themselves what they should do	*11 So they said to him, "What should we do to you that the sea may become calm for us?"--for the sea was becoming increasingly stormy.*
d.2	Jonah tells the sailors what they should do (he remains passive)	*12 He said to them, "Pick me up and throw me into the sea. Then the sea will become calm for you, for I know that on account of me this great storm has come upon you."*
c.2	Sailors' physical efforts	*13 However, the men rowed desperately to return to land but they could not, for the sea was becoming even stormier against them..*
b.2	Pagans pray to God	*14 Then they called on the LORD and said, "We earnestly pray, O LORD, do not let us perish on account of this man's life and do not put innocent blood on us; for You, O LORD, have done as You have pleased."*
a.2	End of the storm and the sailors' fear	*15 So they picked up Jonah, threw him into the sea, and the sea stopped its raging. 16Then the men **feared** the LORD **greatly**, and they offered a sacrifice to the LORD and made vows.*

Detailed Structure of Section B.2 (4:1-11)

a.1	The angry prophet emphasizes God's compassion	*1 <u>But it greatly displeased Jonah and he became angry</u>.* *2 He prayed to the LORD and said, "Please LORD, was not this what I said while I was still in my own country? Therefore in order to forestall this I fled to Tarshish, for I knew that <u>You are a gracious and compassionate God, slow to anger and abundant in lovingkindness, and one who relents concerning calamity</u>.*
b.1	Jonah wants to die and God admonishes him for his anger	*3 Therefore now, O LORD, please take my life from me,* ***for death is better to me than life."*** ***4 The LORD said, "Do you have good reason to be angry?"***
c.1	Jonah builds a shelter to have some shade. He is active.	*5 Then Jonah went out from the city and sat east of it. There he made a shelter for himself and sat under it in the shade until he could see what would happen in the city.*
d.1	God makes a vine grow	*6 So the LORD God appointed a plant and it grew up over Jonah to be a shade over his head to deliver him from his discomfort.*
e	Jonah's joy	*And Jonah was* ***extremely happy*** *about the plant.*
d.2	God makes the vine wither	*7 But God appointed a worm when dawn came the next day and it attacked the plant and it withered.*
c.2	Jonah suffers under the sun and from the heat. He is weak.	*8 When the sun came up God appointed a scorching east wind, and the sun beat down on Jonah's head so that he became faint*
b.2	Jonah wants to die and God admonishes him for his anger	*and begged with all his soul to die, saying,* ***"Death is better to me than life."*** *9 Then God said to Jonah, "Do you have good reason to be angry about the plant?"*
a.2	God emphasizes his compassion (in the form of a question) to the angry prophet	*And he said, "I have good reason to <u>be angry, even to death</u>."* *Then the LORD said, "You had compassion on the plant for which you did not work and which you did not cause to grow, which came up overnight and perished overnight.* *11 "<u>Should I not have compassion on Nineveh, the great city</u> in which there are more than 120,000 persons who do not know the difference between their right and left hand, as well as many animals?"*

Some keywords of the Biblical text are highlighted (in bold print or underlined). Section B.1 centers on a great fear, whereas in section B.2 the focus is on great joy. The cornerstones of B.1 are also marked by fear; the perimeters of B.2 are marked by the prophet's anger and God's compassion.

The Central Sections: C.1 (1:17-2:10) and C.2 (3:4-10)

At the centre of the book we find the two sections which illustrate the themes of repentance and pardon. In Chapter 2, Jonah witnesses his repentance (2:2-9) and God shows his pardon by sending the fish which swallows Jonah and then spits him out again (1:17; 2:10). In Chapter 3, the Ninevites clothe themselves with all of the outward signs of repentance (3:5-8) and God spares Nineveh from destruction: *"God relented concerning the calamity which He had declared He would bring upon them. And He did not do it."* (3:10). Jonah confesses his repentance verbally and the Ninevites do it with gestures (they never speak to God). Jonah vows to act (*"That which I have vowed I will pay"* 2:9); Nineveh's king exhorts his people to stop committing certain acts *("that each may turn from his wicked way and from the violence which is in his hands."* 3:8).

Communication is excellent. Jonah proclaims that the LORD has heard him (2:2, 7), despite the fact that he is in a place where no further communication is possible (in the realm of the dead, the depths of the sea). When Jonah commits to carrying out his vows (e.g. his mission), God immediately releases him (2:9-10). In Chapter 3, as soon as Jonah utters a few words on the first day, the entire population repents (3:4-5). As for the Ninevites, despite the fact that they do not address God in any way, he understands their message and accepts their repentance.

On the geographical level, Jonah is inside a place in both sections, first inside the fish, then inside the ramparts of Nineveh, a city whose name means "the house of the fish" (see footnote 3, p. 135). Thus, at the centre of the book, Jonah is at the heart of God's will and is surrounded by a protective barrier.

We also note that a period of three days is mentioned in both sections: *"Jonah was in the stomach of the fish three days and three nights."* 1:17; *"Now Nineveh was an exceedingly great city, a three days' walk"* 3:3. The fast of animals is also a characteristic of both sections: in Chapter 2, the fish does not eat Jonah, but merely swallows him (he offers him shelter), and in Chapter 3, the animals cannot nourish themselves *("Do not let man, beast, herd, or flock taste a thing. Do not let them eat or drink water."* 3:7).

The structure of both central sections (C.1 and C.2) is not as detailed as that of the outer sections (B.1 and B.2). It is limited to one text divided into four parts: two borders (introduction and conclusion) and two central parts.

Detailed Structure of Section C.1 (1:17-2:10)

a.1	God sends the fish who saves Jonah, but keeps him prisoner	1:17-2:1
b.1	Jonah praises and thanks his LORD	2:2-7
b.2	Jonah intercedes and commits to carrying out his vow	2:8-9
a.2	God orders the fish to let Jonah go	2:10

Detailed Structure of Section C.2 (3:4-11)

a.1	Jonah announces a great upheaval for Nineveh	3:4
b.1	Commitment of the people and of the king	3:5-6
b.2	Royal decree to impose the commitment on everyone	3:7-9
a.2	God repents and suspends his judgment	3:10

The borders underscore God's redemption (1:17-2:1; 2:10; 3:4, 10) and the centres describe Jonah's and the Ninevites' commitment in detail (2:2-9; 3:5-9). A reader could be disappointed by the textual simplicity of the middle sections compared to the complexity of sections B.1 and B.2. Yet this simplicity does not mean mediocrity. Quite on the contrary, the author expresses the middle sections' change of theme with a change of style. He places two accounts of a particular literary genre at the centre, rather than two accounts organised as a chiasmus. Chapter 2 is written in the form of a poem, (see Commentary, p. 127) and Chapter 3 contains an official Assyrian decree (3:7-9). On the one hand, we have a lively poem of a faithful believer brimming over with *joie de vivre* to express his feelings to his LORD, and on the other an authoritative decree to express a pagan people's commitment.

Concentric Structure Centred on the Psalm

A third structure can be found in the book. It does not take up the division marked by the double call of the LORD, but instead centers on Jonah's psalm, the only poem in the book.[9] The account moves from revolt to submission, then back to revolt.

9 Olivier Fasel, pastor and former Emmaus student, suggested the outline of this structure to me.

A.1	The LORD gives a first order to Jonah: 1:1-2
B.1	Jonah flees from the face of the LORD: 1:3
C.1	The LORD lets a wind blow over the sea and the sailors jettison their cargo; the pagans fear for their lives: 1:4-5a
D.1	Jonah shows suicidal tendencies, but he saves the sailors: 1:5b-12
E.1	The sailors obey the prophet and pray to God; they reject the guilty one (Jonah is thrown into the sea): 1:13-16
F.1	The LORD sends a fish which swallows Jonah and saves him: 1:17
G	Jonah expresses his gratitude to the LORD in the fish: 2:1-9
F.2	The LORD speaks to the fish who spits Jonah out and releases him: 2:10
E.2	The Ninevites welcome the faithful prophet's words and convert (Jonah enters Nineveh): 3
D.2	Jonah says he wants to die and asks God to kill him: 4:1-5
C.2	God sends a hot wind and takes away what he has given Jonah; the prophet gets depressed: 4:6-8a
B.2	Jonah stands firm in a standoff with God: 4:8b-9
A.2	The LORD asks Jonah one last question: 4:10-11

A.1 and A.2: In the test of strength with Jonah, the LORD has both the first and last word.[10] The initial order underlines the mission's main goal (the Ninevites' conversion) and the question at the end emphasizes the second goal (to teach Jonah and the world about God's love).

[10] Overduin (*The Adventures of a Deserter: A Modern Parable from an Ancient Story*, p. 11-12) compares the account to a chess match between God and Jonah in which God makes the first move (he starts it off) and last one (he wins the game).

B.1 and B.2: Jonah first expresses his opposition silently by turning his back, then expresses it verbally by refusing to change his position (he repeats twice what he has already expressed previously 4:3).

C.1 and C.2: The LORD manifests his opposition in a non-verbal manner by means of the wind (*rûah*) rather than the breath (*rûah*) of his word.

D.1 and D.2: Jonah puts pressure on God, first by ignoring the danger which the LORD induces (sleep; preoccupation with the Ninevites' fate, without taking into account the consequences for himself), then by asking God to take his life.

E.1 and E.2: The pagans' conversion to God. Contrary to the prophet, they adopt the proper attitude: they reject the sinner, but welcome the faithful prophet. The sea's fury is calmed and the LORD refrains from harming the Ninevites.

F.1 and F.2: God uses a fish for a double task.

G : A poem emphasizes the re-established communion between Jonah and the LORD. The prophet thanks God for his past and future loyalty, and makes a commitment to keep his promise.

Several Dualities

Several elements in the book of Jonah are presented in pairs. Some have already been shown by the parallels between different structures. A list of the most important pairs is helpful to grasp the importance of this literary characteristic more easily.

- Two calls of the LORD (1:1-2; 3:1-2).
- Two groups of foreigners (the sailors and the Ninevites).
- Two animals (the great fish and the small worm).
- Two destructive winds (to the west and to the east).
- Two voyages "to the ends of the earth" (to Tarshish and to Nineveh).
- Two brief stays in the house of a fish (the fish's stomach and Nineveh).

- Two fortunate shelters for Jonah (hut and vine).
- Two main sections (Chapters 1-2 and 3-4).
- Two literary genres (prose and poetry).
- Two goals of the mission (saving the Ninevites and teaching the world about the extent of God's love).
- Two attitudes of Jonah towards the LORD (gratitude and debate).
- Two characteristics of the LORD (his justice and his love).
- Two reasons for the Ninevites' pardon (repentance of sinners [3:10] and ignorance of God's precepts [4:11]).
- Two meanings to Jonah's sign (stay in the tomb and conversion of pagans: see p. 67).

INTERTEXTUALITY

The Biblical accounts fit into a Scriptural ensemble and the comparison of certain texts or persons can often be quite enriching. This kind of procedure is all the more legitimate because the Hebrew way of thinking thrives on comparisons. Thus, Hebrew authors often constructed their writings upon synonymic or antithetic parallels. This is not only the case with the account of Jonah (see previous chapter), but also a number of other books of the Bible.[1] The comparisons are *internal* when the author compares two accounts of his own book; the accounts are thus often adjacent or equidistant from the centre of the chiasmus. The comparisons are *external* if the author compares one account or one person of his book, even his entire book, to a previous writing or person. An author can also announce a future person or event typologically. This places us in the domain of prophecy, the author not always conscious of the entire extent of his words.

The account of Jonah offers a number of antithetical parallels with two prior accounts in particular: that of the flood and that of Sodom and Gomorrah's destruction. As for Jonah's life, it contrasts with certain episodes of Moses's life and it recalls some characteristics of Elijah's. Jonah also typologically announces the person of Jesus Christ.[2] In summary, Jonah's ministry is a contrast to the flood, the judgment of Sodom and the exodus from Egypt at the time of Moses (the period of the Law), but it is an extension of Elijah's ministry and an anticipation of the ministry of Jesus

---

1 For example, see my commentaries on Judges (p. 35-43), Ruth (p. 55-59), Elijah (p. 59-64), Elisha (p. 41-46), Esther (p. 39-42).

2 Jonah experienced these incidents unknowingly, but it is probable that he partly discerned the consequences afterwards (at any rate, the antithetic parallels to the flood and the judgment of Sodom, the contrasts with Moses and similarities to Elijah), particularly if he was the author of the book (see p. 84).

Christ. This chapter presents a detailed study of these parallels.

1. A Story of an Anti-Flood

The Jonah account is the story of an anti-flood. In Hebrew thinking, comparisons are primarily made on the level of ideas, but sometimes, as we see here, identical terms further reinforce the links between the texts.

God's repentance and the destruction of all flesh. During Noah's time, God sees *(ra'ah)* the great wickedness (*ra'*) of men (Ge 6:5) and he is greatly saddened by it. He regrets *(nacham)* having created man *("The LORD was sorry that He had made man on the earth, and He was grieved in His heart."* Gen 6:6) and decides to destroy all humankind and the animals (*"The LORD said, "I will blot out man whom I have created from the face of the land, from man to animals to creeping things and to birds of the sky; for I am sorry that I have made them.'"* Gen 6:7).

At Jonah's time, the wickedness *(ra')* of a city (and not of the entire world) had "*come up*" (Jon 1:2) to him (i.e. had drawn his gaze). He therefore decides to destroy the city, but when he sees *(ra'ah)* that the inhabitants turn away from their evil *(ra')* ways, he turns away *(nacham)* from his decision (*"God relented concerning the calamity which He had declared He would bring upon them. And He did not do it."* Jon 3:10). God also refrains from destroying Nineveh because of the great number of men and animals (*"Should I not have compassion on Nineveh, the great city in which there are more than 120,000 persons who do not know the difference between their right and left hand, as well as many animals?"* Jon 4:11).

The voyage by ship. God gives Noah instructions for the construction of an immense ark (150m long: Ge 6:15) and tells him to enter it, not for the purpose of taking a trip but simply to be saved from the flood. On the other hand, Jonah decides on his own to undertake a voyage on a large ship (the expression *"the ships of Tarshish"* designates great ships) to show his opposition to God's orders.

Noah's "local" voyage lasts a full year (Ge 7:11; 8:13-16), but Jonah's long voyage all the way to Tarshish is curtailed.

The danger of the waters. God saves Noah from the rain, whereas Jonah risks drowning to death because of a storm sent by God. Noah is saved from the waters from above (cf. Ge 7:11-12) and Jonah is menaced by waters from below. The wind *(rûah)* lowers the waters for Noah (Ge 8:1), but the wind *(rûah)* whips up the waters in Jonah's case (Jon 1:4).

The salvation of men. Noah saves his family members by giving them shelter on the ark; Jonah saves the sailors (e.g. strangers) from the storm by suggesting that they throw him into the sea. Noah does not speak, but acts; Jonah speaks, but does not act (the sailors have to throw him overboard). The pagans of Noah's day are not taken onto the ark and therefore drown; the idol-worshiping sailors who welcome Jonah aboard their ship can stay there, and it is the believer (Jonah) who is thrown into the water.

Pinnacle and abyss. Noah is lifted above the mountain summits (Ge 7:20),[3] whereas Jonah sinks to their roots (Jon 2:6).

The salvation of animals. Noah saves non-aquatic animals *("Of the birds after their kind, and of the animals after their kind, of every creeping thing of the ground after its kind, two of every kind"* Ge 6:20); Jonah is saved by a fish (one of the animal species who did not need to be saved by Noah). On the other hand, the worm (a "reptile" in Biblical terminology) depresses Jonah.

The dove of peace. Noah twice releases a dove. The second time, it comes back with an olive twig, the sign of salvation (Ge 8:8-11). Jonah is the "dove" of God, because that is what his name means. He is told to announce God's message afar, but he does not deliver the message of salvation to the Ninevites until after his second departure (Jon 1:1-3; 3:1-3).

The preachers of righteousness. The apostle Peter mentions that Noah was *"a preacher of righteousness"* (2 Pet 2:5), whereas Jonah was the son of Amitai, e.g. *"the son of*

---

3 Christensen p. 49

truth" (Jon 1:1). Noah preached repentance without success, but Jonah's message was immediately accepted by the entire population (Jon 3).

A period of 40 days. During the flood, judgment lasted 40 days (Gen 7:12), but for the Ninevites, judgment is withheld for 40 days.

Jonah's ministry thus stands in complete contrast to the flood. God no longer manifests his wrath and judgment, but his grace and pardon instead. He wants to offer the Ninevites (who represent the men most distant from the LORD) an occasion to escape final judgment. A similar lesson results from comparing Jonah's account with that of Sodom and Gomorrah's destruction.

2. The Opposite of Sodom's Judgment

Wickedness of the cities. Sodom's and Nineveh's situations appear to be identical. The enormity of their sin has reached God's ears. He will "descend" to see if the news is true (Gen 18:20-21) and the Ninevites' wickedness "has risen" up to God (Jon 1:2). The word "wicked[ness]" (*ra'*) is used to describe both cities (Ge 13:13; Jon 1:2).

Announcement of destruction. Although both cities' sin is great, their respective fates are different. God announces Sodom's destruction to Abraham, but without the slightest hint of salvation. The information is destined only for the patriarch, who does not have to warn the Sodomites of the divine judgment. On the other hand, Jonah is not only informed of Nineveh's fate, but is charged to announce the judgment to the Ninevites to offer them one last opportunity to repent and be saved. In Genesis, the accent is on the information *communicated* to Abraham, whereas in Jonah, it is placed on the information *to be transmitted* by the prophet.

Man's reaction to God. Both men contest the legitimacy of God's action. Abraham feels that the LORD is too severe with Sodom, and Jonah thinks he is too lax with Nineveh. Abraham addresses God and engages in a long appeal to save the city (Ge 18:22-33). Jonah, on the other hand, turns his back and runs *"away from the LORD"*; he does not say anything to the LORD, but instead communicates his opposition non-verbally. God approves each of Abraham's requests, but hardens his tone towards Jonah (1:13), to the point of threatening him with death.

One could possibly believe that Abraham is moved by an impartial care for strangers, but his request was more likely motivated by the presence of his nephew Lot in the impious city. Some feel that Jonah is a xenophobe because he refuses to grant the Ninevites one last chance; yet he is prepared to sacrifice himself to save the sailors (Jon 1:12).

One might also believe that Abraham has a greater love than God, but in the end God saves not only Lot but his closest family members (Ge 19:12-16). One could also think that Jonah is more compassionate than God towards the sailors (because the LORD is getting ready to drown them and the prophet accepts to die to save them). However, the sailors are not innocent, because they received the rebellious prophet and helped him to flee. Jonah does not sacrifice himself for the sailors (because he does not throw himself into the sea) but instead simply expresses a theological principle: he who wishes to escape divine judgment must get rid of his sin.

The fate of the righteous in the city. Abraham intercedes to save a handful of righteous people who live in Sodom (up to ten); God explains to Jonah that he wants to spare Nineveh because of the multitude of men who are too immature to be guilty (*"Nineveh, the great city in which there are more than 120,000 persons who do not know the difference between their right and left hand"* Jon 4:11).

Welcome reserved for God's messengers. The behaviour of the two cities' inhabitants is diametrically opposed. At Sodom, the angels are harassed for no reason, although they are in the guise of simple travellers (Ge 19:1-5). At Nineveh, Jonah, who could have been assaulted after his message of destruction, is listened to and remains unharmed.

Observation of divine judgment on the city. Lot is told to leave the city and not look back when the divine judgment takes place (his wife disobeys and dies on the spot, Ge 19:17, 26). Jonah, on the other hand, installs himself to the east of the city to watch its destruction.

3. Jonah, a New Moses

Moses serves as the standard reference for the Israelites. Now, Jonah presents quite a different picture compared to the great lawgiver. He announces a new stage of God's redemption plan with several contrasts.[4]

Voyage to foreign lands. Both men are called to leave their homes and to go abroad. Moses must definitively guide the Hebrews out of Egypt to lead them to the Promised Land. Jonah, on the other hand, must temporarily leave his people and the Promised Land to go to a pagan nation.

Ministry for Israel and ministry to the nations. Moses is the man of the people, who lives with his people and does everything to save them. Jonah is a man called to a ministry for strangers, and the entire account takes place far from his fellow believers. Jonah lives with pagans in the west (the

[4] Some liberal or pre-millenarian commentators see Jonah as a type of Israel. Feuillet (col. 1120) expresses the liberal point of view: "Jonah rebelling against his mission, is Israel. For this reason, he is beset by calamity (the tempest) and swallowed by this unprecedented catastrophe called exile... Israel is delivered from exile just like Jonah, whom the monster spews onto the shore ... After exile, Israel still has the same mission, and the truth is carried to the Gentiles (Nineveh repents); Jonah throws a fit, it is Israel who obstinately resists God's will." But a post-exile framework for the writing of the book raises a number of questions (see p. 71, 79-80). NDB (1961 edition, p. 408) illustrates the pre-millenarian point of view: "The fish spits Jonah onto the coast of Palestine from whence he departed, and the peoples must throw Israel back onto the shores of its homeland... In the same way, Israel, who has returned to Palestine, will find repentance and a new vocation there to evangelise the pagans, who convert at the sound of his voice (Es 66:18-20; 2:2-4; Zach 8:20-23)." These two "typological" approaches are not very convincing, because they are based on very fragile traits which attempt to link type and archetype.

sailors) and with the pagans of the east (the Ninevites). His only attachment to Israel is shown by his recollection of the temple which he rejoices to see again (Jon 2:4, 7).

Ministry of the law and of grace. One of Moses's major contributions was to transmit God's law to Israel. Jonah would have loved to apply the law of justice, but must announce the law of grace.[5]

Man's pleading to God and the LORD's repentance. Moses pleads for his sinful people to prevent God from destroying the entire nation, and the LORD shows remorse (Ex 32:9-14). On the other side, Jonah seeks the Ninevites' destruction and he contests God's right to repent and to go back on his decision.

The mission's motive. Moses displays a certain impatience to help his people because he protected a Hebrew from oppression by the Egyptians forty years before the LORD called him. Jonah, on the other hand, from start to finish does not wish to help the Ninevites.

Hesitation at the call. Both men express their reservations at the moment of the divine call. Moses resists it with words, because he fears that his people will not listen to him (Ex 4:1, 10). Jonah manifests his reluctance visibly, because he is afraid that the Ninevites will actually listen. But Moses was known by the Hebrews (he had been at the pharao's court), whereas the Ninevites would not have known Jonah.

Flight. At one given moment of their life, both men flee. Moses does it prior to God's call and Jonah flees as a reaction to his call. Moses flees for fear of pharaoh and Jonah flees not out of fear of the Ninevites, which we are led to believe at the book's start, but because of his opposition to God (4:2).

---

[5] The law of Moses was used in Israel to determine the punishment of criminals. However, it also contained measures of grace for repentant sinners. The sacrificial system centered on yom kippur (the great day of atonement) confirmed God's pardon. A change of emphasis can nevertheless be perceived between Moses and Jonah, exactly like the contrast between Moses and Jesus: *"For the law was given through Moses; grace and truth were realized through Jesus Christ."*(Jn 1:17).

Depression. Both men are discouraged and irritated to the point of desiring death (Nb 11:10, 15; Jon 4:3, 8-9); Moses because the LORD is angered at the people's complaints, and Jonah because God pardons the Ninevites who have repented.

Salvation by water. Both men are saved by water (Moses's very name bears the meaning: "because I *drew him out of the water*" Ex 2:10). Moses's parents put him into the Nile to save him (Ex 2:3), and Jonah suggests that he be thrown into the sea to save the sailors (Jon 1:12, 15). Moses is saved by the sweet water of a river (there is neither wind nor rain) and Jonah is saved by the saltwater of the Mediterranean during an exceptionally violent storm. Moses is alone in a tiny vessel; Jonah is surrounded by an entire crew of a large ship. Moses' salvation is confirmed by his sister (Ex 2:4-8), whereas the sailors do not witness Jonah's.

The man of God is welcomed. Moses is heard by his people (who despite this will often oppose him afterwards), but pharaoh does not listen, and becomes increasingly harder. On the other hand, the Ninevites, then their king, immediately pay attention to Jonah.

4. A Complement to Ruth

The book of Jonah shares the theme of foreigners with the book of Ruth. Divine grace does not exclude non-Jews, even the most distant (the Moabites were not allowed to enter the assembly of the LORD [Dt 23:4-7] and the Ninevites were particularly bloodthirsty people). Ruth is the book about giving oneself and of integration into the family of God, whereas Jonah is the book about divine pardon and the absence (or postponement) of divine judgment.[6]

The novelty about the book of Jonah is that the LORD not only welcomes foreigners who come to Israel and are keen on getting to know him, but that he even sends a messenger to reach criminal pagans who know nothing of him. Jonah does the fishing, not with a line from the riverbank, but with a net

6 A detailed comparison between the two accounts can be found in my commentary "*Ruth à la croisée des chemins*" p. 51-52.

from a boat which lies in deep water, at a place where there is a large school of fat fish (cf. Jn 21:1-11).

5. Jonah, Elijah's Successor

The ministries of Elijah and Jonah have several similarities, but prior to indicating them, it is first necessary to examine the chronological proximity of the two prophets.

The Period of Elijah, Elisha and Jonah

Jonah appears to be a contemporary of Elisha (who is Elijah's successor) because Elisha dies during the reign of Joash, king of Israel (2 Kings 13:14-21) and Jonah prophesied during the reign of Jeroboam II, Joash's successor (2 Kings 14:25). Jewish tradition teaches that Jonah was a disciple of Elisha, which is possible, as the latter lived among his people and was often surrounded by servants (2 Kings 4:12; 5:10, 20; 6:15; 9:1). Furthermore, both men came from the northern kingdom and carried out their ministry in that region (1 Kings 19:16; 2 Kings 14:25). It could also be that Jonah was born whilst Elijah was still carrying out his prophetic ministry in Israel.[7]

This period of Israel's history is characterised by an increasingly obvious revelation of divine grace towards pagans through the prophetic acts of Elijah, Elisha and Jonah. The first brings the son of the Sarepta widow back to life, which is grace manifested towards a pagan, but the good deed could be interpreted as a service rendered by the prophet towards the widow because of her hospitality. At first, Elijah resents the fact that the LORD has let the child of a woman who has been so generous to him die: *"O LORD my God,*

---

[7] According to Jewish tradition, Jonah was the son of the Shunammite whom Elijah had brought back to life (Scherman p. xvii). Actually, Jonah is the son of Amittai ("the truth") and after the resurrection of her child, the widow recognized that *the truth* was in Elijah's words *("Now I know that you are a man of God and that the word of the LORD in your mouth is the truth."* 1 Kings 17:24). This comparison is rather weak.

have you also brought calamity to the widow with whom I am staying, by causing her son to die?" (1 Kings 17:20).

Elisha heals Naaman, the Syrian. This time, there is no doubt about grace, as the prophet has no debt to repay to the general. Quite on the contrary, he could have resented him for having waged war against Israel and keeping a young Israelite as a slave (2 Kings 5:2). Nevertheless, Elisha heals the pagan without seeking the slightest financial compensation (the text with the episode regarding Guehazi specifically emphasizes this: 2 Kings 5:20-27) or political favour (the prophet does not request the return of the Israelite slaves held by the Syrians). One must, however, recognize that Naaman is a generous man and is prepared to commit himself in faith. Later on, Elisha feeds and frees a Syrian army who is intent on harming him (2 Kings 6:22). The grace towards the pagans is obvious because Elisha is benevolent towards his enemies. However, the Syrian troops' evil intentions were limited, because they certainly had no intention of killing Elisha; they only wished to capture him and use him as a collaborator.[8]

With Jonah, God's love enters a new stage. Now it is no longer simply a question of welcoming pagans, but of giving grace to the worst sinners. Jonah must go to a bloodthirsty city to express the full scope of God's love. The book of Kings also informs us that Jonah had prophesied the success of the Israelite troops despite the fact that their king, Jeroboam II *"did evil in the sight of the LORD, he did not depart from all the sins of Jeroboam the son of Nebat, which he made Israel sin."* (2 Kings 14:24). It is grace to its full extent. The LORD has pity on a sinful people who suffers profoundly: *"For the LORD saw the affliction of Israel, which was very bitter; for there was neither bond nor free, nor was there any helper for Israel. The LORD did not say that He would blot out the name of Israel from under heaven, but He saved them by the hand of Jeroboam the son of Joash."* (2 Kings 14:26-27).

---

8 D. Arnold, *Elisée, précurseur de Jésus-Christ*, p. 142.

The Ministries of Elijah and Jonah

Thus, Jonah's ministry fits both chronologically and thematically into the legacies of Elijah and Elisha, but the similarities to the ministry of Elijah, the prophet of judgment, are particularly striking.

Courage. Both men must appear before a perverse political authority whom they are to reprimand. They are not discouraged by the mission's difficulty nor its inherent dangers. Elijah immediately goes to Ahab to announce the drought (1 Kings 17:1) and Jonah also accomplishes his mission (Jon 3:3-4). If Amittai's son does not obey immediately, it is not because he fears the Ninevites (Jon 4:2), but rather because he refuses to extend God's grace to those sinners.

Flight. Both prophets flee at a certain point. Elijah even does so twice: first upon God's order (1 Kings 17:2-3), then because of his perspicacity (1 Kings 19:3).[9] Jonah flees to give evidence of his displeasure with God. In all three cases, fear is not the reason for flight.

God's support through animals. The LORD assists both prophets in their task by using animals. He sends crows to feed Elijah after he has carried out his mission (1 Kings 17:4, 6) and a fish to save Jonah before he accomplishes his mission (Jon 1:17; 2:10). In both cases, the animals do not eat what they should have eaten (the bread on the one hand and Jonah on the other).

Devastating discouragement after a successful mission. Both prophets sink into depression, to the point of wanting to die, after having completed their mission and having succeeded in convincing many people. Elijah had convinced the Israelites of God's sovereignty (*"When all the people saw it, they fell on their faces; and they said, 'The LORD, He is God; the LORD, He is God!'"* 1 Kings 18:39) and Jonah leads the Ninevites to confess their sins (Jon 3:5-9). Despite this, after these successes, both prophets turn suicidal: Elijah

---

[9] The correct translation is: *"Seeing this, Elijah, ..."* and not *"Elijah, being frightened, ..."*: see D. Arnold, *Elie entre le jugement et la grâce*, p. 111-112.

"requested for himself that he might die, and said, 'It is enough; now, O LORD, take my life, for I am not better than my fathers.'" (1 Kings 19:4) and Jonah says: *"Therefore now, O LORD, please take my life from me, for death is better to me than life"* (Jon 4:3, 8).

Difficulty with giving grace to sinners. Elijah is miserable because the LORD hesitates so long to punish Ahab,[10] and Jonah is irritated by the fact that the LORD pardons the Ninevites (Jon 4:1-2).

Instruction by a double interrogation. The LORD tries to instruct his two prophets on the theme of grace, but faced with their problems of comprehension, he resorts to a question which he asks twice using the same words. He asks Elijah: *"What are you doing here?"* (1 Kings 19:9, 13) and Jonah: *"Do you have good reason to be angry?"* (Jon 4:4, 9). The prophets' replies reflect their lack of understanding. Elijah restricts himself to describing his defeat twice, in the same terms (1 Kings 19:10, 14) and Jonah stubbornly justifies his attitude: *"'I have good reason to be angry, even to death.'"* (Jon 4:9).

Announcement of a final judgment which is postponed. Both prophets announce a judgment which appears irrevocable, but which ends up being postponed or cancelled altogether due to the offenders' repentance. Ahab himself escapes the judgment pronounced upon his dynasty (1 Kings 21:17-29) and the Ninevites are given grace after repenting (Jon 3:10). Neither of the prophets of judgment was apparently asked–or else they felt it unnecessary–to inform the wrongdoers of the divine pardon granted.

Conclusion

Jonah and Elijah behave in a similar fashion. It is obvious that both men find it difficult to accept the extent of divine grace. Some may judge Jonah more severely than Elijah because the son of Amittai had already benefited from both Elijah's and Elisha's teachings on divine grace. And a pioneer's progress is always more laborious than that of his

10 *Elie entre le jugement et la grâce*, p. 113-120.

successors. Nonetheless, Jonah not only followed his two predecessors, but also surpassed them in his proclamation of God's love. Through Jonah's ministry, God announces the extent of his love for sinners of every nation like he never has before.

6. An Example for Jeremiah's Contemporaries

What impact did Jonah leave on Israel? It is difficult to say exactly, but it seems that Jeremiah was not indifferent to the ministry of Amittai's son. In fact, Chapter 36 of his book seems to echo the book of Jonah (particularly Chapter 3). The themes of judgment, repentance and pardon are particularly emphasized. Jeremiah must announce judgment upon Israel, who has separated itself from the LORD. But contrary to the king of Nineveh, Israel's king does not repent.

Everything has begun well at the start, because the message is read on a day of fasting, and both the people as well as the elders are frightened (Jer 36:16). Yet king Jehoiakim does not follow either his people's or the king of Nineveh's example. Instead of issuing an edict, proclaiming a general fast, displaying all the signs of repentance and tearing his garments, he calmly cuts the message sent by Jeremiah into little pieces, page by page.

The whole situation is reversed in Judah. From the start, Jeremiah risks a great danger because he proclaims his message to the king (contrary to Jonah, who was not harmed in any way by the Ninevites). He must hide and transmit the message in writing through an intermediary. Even Baruch, the bearer of the message, must hide afterwards.[11]

The fundamental question is not if God will pardon the repentant sinner. The king of Nineveh in fact ends his edict with the following reflection: "*Who knows, God may turn and relent and withdraw His burning anger so that we will not*

---

[11] Elsewhere in Jeremiah there is a warning against killing a prophet and spilling innocent blood (Je 26:15; cf. Jon 1:14).

perish." (Jon 3:9). In Jeremiah's day, the LORD confirms loudly and strongly that he will pardon the repentant sinner, but the basic question is about knowing if Israel will repent or not: *"Perhaps the house of Judah will hear all the calamity which I plan to bring on them, in order that every man will turn from his evil way; then I will forgive their iniquity and their sin."* (Je 36:3, cf. v.7).

Before we close our remarks on Jeremiah, we would like to draw attention to the fact that the only Old Testament book which mentions Jonah apart from the book of Jonah is the book of 1-2 Kings. Jewish tradition attributes the authorship of the book to Jeremiah. Several clues support this hypothesis:

1. The book of 1-2 Kings does not mention Jeremiah, which is surprising, as the narrator is strongly interested in prophets, and Jeremiah is the main prophet at the end of the period of royalty and the beginning of the exile, the period during which 1-2 Kings was written. Such an omission can only be explained if we suppose that the author does not mention himself out of modesty.
2. The last Chapter of 1-2 Kings is practically identical to the last chapter of Jeremiah. Couldn't this be a way in which Jeremiah "signed" the book of Kings?
3. The book of 1-2 Kings exudes a prophetic spirit. Prophets have a predominant position. Their announcements and the analysis of Samaria's fall (2 Kings 17) are in a symbiosis with Jeremiah's prophetic exhortations.

In conclusion, if Jeremiah wrote 1-2 Kings, the inclusion of Jonah in the book would confirm the attention which Jonah receives from Jeremiah. The latter, more than any other prophet, might have regretted his people's hardening, particularly in comparison with the spiritual openness of the Ninevites.

7. Jonah, a Type of Jesus Christ

Two aspects of Jesus's ministry are announced typologically by Jonah: the passion and the universal ministry of salvation. The Gospel of Matthew, incidentally, mentions two of the signs in Jonah: the time in the fish and the Ninevites' repentance (Mt 12:38-41). But before considering these two aspects, it is helpful to take a look at the links which Jesus makes between himself and Jonah, as well as both men's geographical proximity.[12]

Origin and Identification

Jesus and Jonah come from the same geographical area, because Gath-Hepher is located only five kilometres northeast of Nazareth (*NCB* p. 782). The Pharisees of Jerusalem ignored this information when they reproached Nicodemus for defending Jesus: *"They replied, 'Are you from Galilee, too? Look into it, and you will find that a prophet does not come out of Galilee.'"* (Jn 7:52). These doubters quite obviously did not examine Scripture thoroughly enough (cf. Jn 5:39)![13]

---

[12] Some commentators draw attention to Jonah's messianic typology: Gaebelin p. 122-124, Guers p. 9-12. Others underline the contrasts instead. According to R.T. France, one needs to understand that "At other points there is contrast rather than correspondence, in that Jonah was 'imprisoned' as a punishment for disobedience, and as the beginning of his effective ministry, which led to the repentance of his listeners, whereas Jesus' death and resurrection were the culmination of a ministry of utter obedience, yet one which met with little acceptance. But typology does not depend on equivalence at every point, and Jesus's 'argument' establishes the correspondence in what was, for the Jew, the essential point of the story of Jonah" (p. 45). Thus, Joseph announces Christ's rejection by his brothers as well as his future glory, Elisha announces Jesus's earthly healing ministry (but not the passion), Jonah announces Christ's death/resurrection and the work of the Holy Spirit as from Pentecost. See D. Arnold, *Elisée précurseur de Jésus-Christ*, p. 26-30, 137-139.

[13] Prior to Christ's death, the Pharisees were not able to make as many connections as a reader of the Gospels could, but they could at least have remembered Jonah, the persuasive preacher, seeing as they did

Jesus Christ identified himself with seven persons from the Old Testament: Abraham,[14] Moses,[15] David,[16] Solomon,[17] Elijah,[18] Elisha[19] and Jonah[20]. In general, he emphasises his superiority with regard to these illustrious ancestors, but he never uses the expression "the same" (*hôs*) except with Jonah.

Jesus speaks of a "sign of Jonah" three times (Mt 12:38-41; 16:4; Lk 11:29-32), and each time it is in a context of disbelief.[21] Every one of these times, Jesus refuses to respond to the Pharisees' demand for miraculous signs, and simply refers them to the "sign of Jonah". The two miracles to which these signs refer in particular illustrate Christ's power *after the crucifixion*. The sign of the "three days and three nights" announces Christ's resurrection and that of the Ninevites' repentance proclaims the mass conversion of pagans. Jesus

---

observe that Jesus was a convincing speaker: *"Finally the temple guards went back to the chief priests and Pharisees, who asked them, 'Why didn't you bring him in?' 'No one ever spoke the way this man does,' the guards declared."* (Jn 7:45-46).

14 Jn 8:53-58.

15 Jn 3:14; 5:46; 6:30-35; 7:21-23.

16 Mt 12:3; 22:42-45; and the parallels in Mk and Lk.

17 Mt 12:42; Lk 11:31.

18 Lk 4:25-26.

19 Lk 4:27.

20 Mt 12:40-41; 16:4; Lk 11:29-30.

21 The reference in Luke is chronologically different from those in Matthew. (1) Mt 12:38-41 takes place in the first part of the Galilean ministry (just before the great speech on the parables in Mt 13). (2) Mt 16:4 is at the end of the Galilean ministry, after the second multiplication of bread. (3) Lk 11:29-32 takes place during "Jesus's long journey to Jerusalem" (Lk 9:51-19:28), probably during one of Jesus's stays in Jerusalem during the feast of Tabernacles, six months prior to his death (Jn 7:2-13; in Lk 10:38-42, Jesus is in the house of Martha and Mary who lived in Bethany, 3 km from Jerusalem).

In Mt 12 and in Lk 11, the mention of the sign immediately follows a reference regarding sins against the Holy Spirit, e.g. rejection of Christ despite the evident signs of his Messianic nature (his is accused of driving out mute demons by the power of the devil). In Mt 16, Jesus experiences general disbelief, particularly by the Pharisees and Sadducees, just after carrying out the second multiplication of bread, i.e. after a second public witness in front of thousands of people.

thus refuses to show the Pharisees other miracles of healing or relief of physical discomfort (multiplication of bread), and refers them to two great miracles which follow the crucifixion: resurrection of the Messiah and the sending of the Holy Spirit to lead people to the faith.

Announcement of Jesus's Passion

Jonah's time inside the fish is directly linked to Christ's death.

Three days and three nights. The duration of the stay is the most obvious detail, because it is revealed by Jesus himself: *"For as Jonah was three days and three nights in the belly of the sea monster, so will the Son of Man be three days and three nights in the heart of the earth"* (Mt 12:40; cf. Jon 1:17).[22] Both men's situation was desperate and only God was able to save them by a miracle. But there are other elements which connect these two events.

The sacrifice of a prophet to save mankind. Jonah tells the sailors to throw him into the sea to calm the storm, but he does not throw himself in; Jesus accepts being arrested, sentenced and crucified without offering the slightest resistance and without a word of defense, despite the fact that he had all wisdom and knowledge to counter his enemies and all heavenly powers at his disposal to defend himself physically. Jesus and Jonah remain passive within the salvation they offer.

Vain efforts by pagans to save the prophet. Before they throw Jonah into the sea, the sailors increase their efforts to rescue him (Jon 1:13). Before he delivers Jesus to the Jews, Pontius Pilate made an effort to save him. The sailors finally give up *"for the sea was becoming even stormier against them."* (Jon 1:13). Pilate gives in after the Jews accuse him of betraying the emperor: *"If you release this Man, you are no friend of Caesar; everyone who makes himself out to be a king opposes Caesar."* (Jn 19:12).

---

[22] For the exact duration of time between Jesus's death and his resurrection, see footnote 5 p. 106.

Sent to the abyss by sinners. Jonah is thrown into the Mediterranean; Jesus is delivered into the hands of the Roman authorities (the masters of the Mediterranean). Symbolically, the Mediterranean (also called "the great sea") represents the pagan world (cf. Da 7:2-3; Rev 12:18; 13:1).

God's hidden miracle. The sailors think that Jonah is dead and that his mission to the Ninevites has failed. The sailors probably did not see the fish swallow Jonah, and even if they had, they could not have imagined that it would release the prophet, alive, on the edge of the shore.

The onlookers at the crucifixion had every reason to believe that Jesus had failed his mission. They did not realize that the great victory over evil had been won when Jesus had cried out: *"It is finished"* (Jn 19:30) just before passing away. In the same way, these men saw nothing of the resurrection.

The signs linked to death create life. The prophet's "death" is accompanied by a certain number of signs which lead the pagans to be open to God. The calming of the storm impresses the sailors and prompts them to seek divine pardon: *"At this the men greatly feared the LORD, and they offered a sacrifice to the LORD and made vows to him."* (Jon 1:16). The signs at the time of the crucifixion are even more apparent:

> *"And Jesus cried out again with a loud voice, and yielded up His spirit. And behold, the veil of the temple was torn in two from top to bottom; and the earth shook and the rocks were split. The tombs were opened, and many bodies of the saints who had fallen asleep were raised; and coming out of the tombs after His resurrection they entered the holy city and appeared to many. Now the centurion, and those who were with him keeping guard over Jesus, when they saw the earthquake and the things that were happening, became very frightened and said, "Truly this was the Son of God!" (Mt 27:50-54).*

The prophet's agony before death. Before sacrificing their life for mankind, the two prophets struggle to accept God's will. Jonah first opposes God by fleeing to Tarshish, then turns a deaf ear to the storm when he is on the ship. In the garden of Gethsemane, Jesus has difficulty to fully accept God's plan; his physical distress indicates the intensity of his struggle: *"And being in agony He was praying very fervently; and His sweat became like drops of blood, falling down upon the ground."* (Lk 22:44).

The prophet's agony at the moment of death. In his psalm, Jonah expresses the anguish which surrounds him at the bottom of the sea. Regarding God, he says *"I have been expelled from Your sight"* (Jon 2:4). Jesus cries out on the cross: *"My God, my God, why have you forsaken me?"* (Mt 27:46).

The wages of sin is death. Jonah was to die because of his rebellion, and Jesus was to die for the sins of man. In both cases, the sanction appears to be severe or futile. The punishment inflicted upon Jonah seems disproportionate, because the prophet did not break any commandment of Mosaic law. As to Christ's substitutionary death, it is not popular amongst contemporary theologians, who prefer to speak about God's love instead of expiation.

Deliverance from death. Jonah was able to continue living due to his repentance, and Jesus was resurrected, because death was unable to imprison the saint of God.

"There is a very striking parallel to Jonah's testimony ('But you brought my life up from the pit' v. 7), in v. 10 of Psalm 16 quoted by Peter in Acts 2:27: 'because you will not abandon me to the grave, nor will you let your Holy One see decay.'" (*NCB* p. 784).

Announcement of the Universal Ministry of Salvation

The Ninevites' conversion is the second "sign of Jonah", as stated by Jesus:[23]

> *"As the crowds were increasing, He began to say, 'This generation is a wicked generation; it seeks for a sign, and yet no sign will be given to it but the sign of*

[23] The book of Matthew mentions the two signs of Jonah: the stay inside of the fish (Mt 12:40) and the Ninivites' repentance (Mt 12:41). Luke mentions only the second sign (Lk 11:29-30, 32).

> *Jonah. "For just as Jonah became a sign to the Ninevites, so will the Son of Man be to this generation... The men of Nineveh will stand up with this generation at the judgment and condemn it, because they repented at the preaching of Jonah; and behold, something greater than Jonah is here.'" (Lk 11:29-32).*

Unique ministry of salvation. Jonah and Jesus are committed to a unique ministry of salvation, a last-chance affair. No other man except Jonah was asked to bear such a message to a pagan people. Jesus thus also initiated a new stage in God's plan. He is the bread of life and the light of men. He is *the* chance of salvation offered to man, because "no-one comes to the Father except through him."

> *"For God so loved the world, that He gave His only begotten Son, that whoever believes in Him shall not perish, but have eternal life. For God did not send the Son into the world to judge the world, but that the world might be saved through Him. He who believes in Him is not judged; he who does not believe has been judged already, because he has not believed in the name of (the only begotten Son of God. " (John 3:16-18).*

Pagans chosen by God. Salvation is announced to the pagans chosen by God. The Ninevites are the only pagans in foreign lands to have received the privilege of hearing the message of salvation. The message of the Gospel was spread for the first time in the first century of our times. The message, accompanied by the powerful action of the Holy Spirit, attracts to God all who are *"appointed for eternal life"* (Ac 13:48).[24]

Mass conversion of pagans. The speed and number of conversions are phenomenal. Only the working of the Holy Spirit can explain the conversion of the Ninevites and that of the 3000 persons at Pentecost. We also note that the number of Nineveh's inhabitants is 120,000 (Jon 4:11). This number is historical (see p. 162-163), but it also represents a perfect number (12 x 100 x 100). It reminds of or announces other

---

24 Our view clearly advocates the doctrine of election.

perfect numbers which represent the total number of the chosen: the 7000 believers of Elijah's day (1 Kings 19:18), the 144,000 martyrs of the Apocalypse (12 x 12 x 10 x 10 x 10: Ap 7:4-8) and the 153 large fish miraculously caught and brought to the shore where the resurrected Christ stands (Jn 21:11).[25]

A call to repentance and salvation. The two aspects are inseparable. Jonah announces "*Nineveh will be overthrown*" (Jon 3:4), which can be understood either as destruction or a complete and positive turnaround (p. 137). Jesus begins by repeating John the Baptist's preaching on repentance (Mt 3:2; 4:17) before emphasizing pardon.

Mass conversion after leaving the tomb. The life-giving message is brought at the exit from the "tomb". Jonah bears his message to the Ninevites after spending three days in the fish, and the good news about Jesus Christ is remarkably well-received after his resurrection and ascension. Only after Christ has returned to his Father do men convert in droves.

Characteristics of the Preachers

An insignificant preacher. Jonah preaches his message unwillingly and nothing distinguishes him from other itinerant preachers (see p. 140). Jesus did not draw attention either; Isaiah's prophecy about this aspect is well-known:

> *"For He grew up before Him like a tender shoot, and like a root out of parched ground; He has no stately form or majesty that we should look upon Him, nor appearance that we should be attracted to Him. He was despised and forsaken of men, a man of sorrows and acquainted with grief; and like one from whom men hide their face , he was despised, and we did not esteem Him." (Is 53:2-3).*

A sermon to the pagans at first refused. At the beginning, Jonah refuses to go to Nineveh, and Jesus refuses

---

[25] Alfred Kuen, *Encyclopédie des difficultés bibliques: Évangiles et Actes*, p. 617-618.

to carry out his ministry to an international audience prior to his passion. For example, when he is in the area of Tyre and Sidon, in non-Jewish territory, he refers to the limited nature of his ministry when refusing to heal a mother's child: *"He answered, 'I was sent only to the lost sheep of the house of Israel.'"* (Mt 15:24). Of course, Jesus does eventually heal the girl, but he does it discreetly, inside a house (Mk 7:24), far from the crowds, and at a distance from the child to prevent anyone from ascertaining how easily the healing is performed.

The dove sent as a witness. Jonah is the "dove" (we recall that this is what his name means) sent to the Ninevites, and Holy Spirit descends upon Jesus in the form of a dove at his baptism (Mt 3:16; Mk 1:10; Lk 3:22; Jn 1:32). Following this, the Holy Spirit plays a fundamental role in the growth of the church.

Sleeping in a boat during a storm. Jonah goes to sleep in the ship's hold when the storm starts (Jon 1:5) and Jesus sleeps on deck when the disciples set sail during a storm on the lake of Galilee (Mk 4:38); both men, who are woken up by the captain and the disciples respectively, calm the storm with their words in order to save their companions. Jonah advises the sailors to throw him overboard, and Jesus commands the wind and the sea to stop raging.

Both men's characteristics. Jonah shows that he possesses many qualities: courage, knowledge of God, faith, truth, perseverance and love of his fellow man (p. 25-31). He thus proclaims the one who completely surpasses him, because Jesus is perfect in all things (Heb 4:15).

THE HISTORICITY OF JONAH'S ACCOUNT

The historicity of the book of Jonah is violently attacked by some commentators, but it is defended just as vigourously by others. The former find it impossible for the account to be historical, and for the latter, it is impossible that it is not.

The stakes of the debate are important. Those who reject the historicity seek to remove an obstruction to human reason, and those who defend it are saddened by the disbelief which lowers faith to the level of human reason. Must Jonah be freed from a literal reading which ignores the literary characteristics of the book, or should one spare Jonah from a critical reading which puts divine revelation into a melting-pot, leaving only the dross to be considered worthy of contemplation by human reason?

We shall begin by depicting the arguments which have led modern-day critics to reject the book's historicity and shall then develop a critic of those arguments. Throughout the discussion, we shall endeavour to pair faith with reason, i.e. to follow a procedure which at the same time refuses both the dictate of human reason as well as desperate flights of irrationality. The Word of God is divine revelation, but it is a message which addresses the human being as a whole, including his intelligence.

1. The Rejection of Historicity

Many modern commentators reject Jonah's historicity. Already in 1967, Bickerman took pains to find a recent book which defended the contrary: "Despite the embarrassment which our story provokes in the believer, its literal historicity is propounded in a Catholic encyclopedia as late as 1956. A Protestant Bible dictionary of 1962 does the same, albeit with some reticence."[1] Although the author appears to restrict his research to certain circles, the opinion he expresses reflects the feelings of many theologians who feel that Jonah's non-historicity is established and that the matter is settled once and for all.[2]

Unacceptable Miracles

In the 19th and 20th centuries, miracles were primarily cited as objections to historicity. How could a rationalist mind accept Jonah's stay inside the fish and the almost instantaneous conversion of the Ninevites? The existence of other mythological accounts about fish and men were raised. Scepticism led some to imagine different situations to describe the original event which had led to the myth of the fish: 1. Jonah was carried on the back of a sea monster. 2. Jonah floated on the cadaver of a fish. 3. The entire episode was a dream. 4. The prophet, who had been thrown from the ship, was rescued by another vessel whose name was *The Whale,* and whose stern was decorated with an effigy of that animal. 5. It was even proposed that after having been shipwrecked, Jonah had stayed at an inn called *The Whale*. A. Feuillet, who also rejects the historicity of the account, nevertheless condemns such mockery: "These kinds of explanations are not even worth refuting."[3]

Others critics mention the impossibility of a prolonged stay inside a fish (lack of air, the gastric acid in the fish's stomach). We are also reminded that a whale eats plankton and is incapable of swallowing large prey due to its narrow gullet.

As for the Ninevites' repentance, it is simply absent in secular history. The critics state that nothing in history leads us to assume that the Ninevites became Jewish.

---

1 Quoted by Lacocque p. 34.

2 For Holbert (p. 59), "To ask the historical question of Jonah is to ask the wrong question."

3 Feuillet col. 1118.

Literary Characteristics of a Story

From the end of the 20th century, the rejection of historicity rests mainly on literary arguments. For Lacocque (p. 34), "The (literary) genre should determine if we are dealing with history or fiction." The book of Jonah is a parable, a satire or "a midrash, a narrative with an historical air which bears a religious teaching" (Chary p. 464).

The fantasmagorical aspect of the narrative is evoked as the main proof of the account's non-historicity. "It is all passing strange. We are in wonderland"[4] "One cannot help observing that the wonders are multiplied at will… It is not so much their strangeness as the lack of proportion between the means and the end which is disconcerting for the believing reader." (Feuillet col. 1114). "In fact, this little book is a series of surprises; it is crammed with an accumulation of hair-raising and eye-popping phenomena, one after the other. The violent seastorm, the submarinelike fish in which Jonah survives as he composes a song, the mass conversion of Nineveh, the magic plant… the bombardment of the reader with surprise after surprise in a provocative manner suggests the author's intention is other than simply to describe historical facts"[5] Jeanneret (p. 4) states that Luther already said: "If the book of Jonah wasn't part of the Bible, everyone would think it was a fairy tale." For Legrand (p. 23), "the author accumulates implausibilities and the reader/listener is not fooled… ."

A number of improbabilities are raised. "The hero is presented as being motivated by passion to the point of madness, which leads him, for example, to wish for death by suicide… Jonah, the prophet, acts like a heathen, the sailors behave like saints, the sea monster is like a 'nautical taxi', the king of Nineveh covers himself with sackcloth and ashes, a band of felons converts and repents…" (Lacocque p. 70).[6] The irony is recognized by many authors.[7]

---

4 Bewer quoted by Alexander in "Jonah and Genre" p. 45.

5 Allen p. 176 quoted by Wiseman p. 33.

6 One can also quote Feuillet (col. 1114-1115): "Never before had any prophet received such a mission amongst heathens, not even Jeremiah,

Orth (p. 275) mentions that the account's historicity and a satirical reading are mutually exclusive. In fact, the satirical dimension can only be considered in the degree that Jonah is viewed as a fictitious character. "Only one reading is destroyed by reading Jonah as parody; this is the 'naive' or 'historical' school, which teaches a literal prophet from the reign of Jeroboam II– but then, all but a few other modern interpretations deny this reading too." The same author also observes that the satirical approach was greatly ignored by the Jews and Christians in the past: "...if the book of Jonah was written as a parody, we may wish to judge it a historical failure... religious readers have largely ignored its irony for over 2000 years."[8]

---

who had been 'appointed as a prophet to the nations' (Jer 1:5). How could Jonah possibly imagine that he could escape from God?... When a storm rises, is it normal for sailors to put the blame on one of the passengers, as if such events were rare on the Mediterranean? Finally, what are we to think of Jonah's psychology? Just beforehand, he is not particularly enthusiastic at the LORD's call, and now he is quick to offer to sacrifice himself to save his companions?... In the same way, hardly has Jonah, the stranger, announced the total destruction of the capital, that the Ninivites both large and small, i.e. approximately one million people, display the most extraordinary signs of repentance. The text is formal on this point: the movement was widespread, without any opposition, neither from the highest magistrates nor from the council of priests. The king himself descends from his throne, and puts on sackcloth and ashes."

7 One could quote A. & P.-E Lacocque (*Le complexe de Jonah. Une étude psycho-religieuse du prophet*, 1989, 320 p.); John C. Holbert ("'Deliverance belongs to Yahweh': Satire in the Book of Jonah", 1981, p. 59-81); John R. Miles ("Laughing at the Bible: Jonah as Parody" in *On Humour and the Comic in the Hebrew Bible*, 1990, p. 202-215); Michael Orth ("Genre in Jonah: The Effects of Parody in the Book of Jonah", 1990, p. 257-281); I.J.J. Spangenberg ("Jonah and Qohelet: Satire Versus Irony", 1996, p. 495-511). In his book *"Irony in the Old Testament"*, Edwin Good quotes Jonah as being a first example of irony.

8 Orth p. 264. Person (p. 153 footnote 63), "The only pre-twentieth-century commentary who understands the book of Jonah as satirical is, to my knowledge."

Insufficient Historical Elements

The absence of many historical details would make the account more of a parable. In particular, the author omits the name of Nineveh's king and all references to the period concerned.[9] For Feuillet and others, a true historian would not have failed to provide several historical details.

On the other hand, the reference to Jonah, a recognised historical person (cf. 2 Kings 14:25), is relativised: "a ring of authenticity... All the story needs is an air of authenticity, not exact historical details" (Dell p. 88). "Certainly the story is set out in a narrative form, but 'all parables resemble a record of historical events" (Allen p. 179). "Neither Jesus nor Matthew emphasized the historical character of the event quoted; that would be as if a scientist today would say: 'You are fighting windmills, just like Don Quixote did'" (Robert North p. 132). Even Jonah's name (dove, i.e. "homeloving") would explain his presence in the account: "It is one of the pieces of information which would probably permit the development of the midrash genre."[10]

A Post-Exile Political Treatise?

After rejecting the historical framework of the 8th century, critics assert that book was written in the 5th century, as a reaction to the centralistic policy of Ezra and Nehemiah. Jonah would be a polemic treatise which underscores the universality of God's love.

"Jonah was written around 430 B.C. as an allegory with a semi-historical aspect and for the purpose of opposing the 'strict nationalism' of the Jewish leaders such as Ezra and Nehemiah ... Following this concept, one can interpret the 'allegory' of Jonah as follows: Jonah represents disobedient

---

9 "Several factors immediately militate against historicity. Smart remarks the complete absence of historical data in the book. The king of Nineveh remains anonymous; he is simply called 'king of Nineveh', which is unusual in the Bible and the annals of the ancient Middle East." (Lacocque p. 34).

10 A. Gelin in A. Feuillet, *Introduction à la Bible*, Tournai, Desclée, 1959, p. 575.

Israel; the sea indicates the pagans; the great fish symbolizes the neo-Babylonian empire, and the three days which Jonah spends in the animal's belly represent the Babylonian captivity."[11] One could add that the fish's regurgitation of Jonah could mean the return from exile and another opportunity given to Israel to display its faith to the surrounding heathen nations.

The chosen historical framework corresponds to the ideas about the evolution of religious thinking which the liberals devise. Because the book of Jonah emphasizes the universality of God's love, the book must be of a later and consequently post-exile date.

Some commentators also detect certain Aramaic terms in the text, which to them would be the sign of a post-exile writing.[12] According to Feuillet (col. 1105), "the language points to a recent period".

Historical Errors

The divergence between the assumed period of the events (the reign of Jeroboam II) and the date of writing would explain several historical errors. In fact, the 5th-century narrator would not have been very familiar with the historical context of the 8th century.

Thus, Nineveh's size would have been underestimated, because no city at that time had a diameter or even a periphery which required a three days' walk to be circumvented, nor did any population reach 120,000.

The reference to the king of Nineveh is also inexact, because in Assyria the cities were presided over by governors and not kings. Only the country as a whole had a king, and Nineveh was not the capital of the Assyrian empire at the beginning of the 8th century; it did not receive that standing until after the death of Sargon II in 705.

---

11 Description of the liberal position by Archer, *A Survey of Old Testament Introduction*, p. 296.

12 Allen p. 186-188.

2. The Defense of Historicity

The Testimony of Jews and the Church for More than 2000 Years

Until the 19th century, Jewish and Christian authors almost always considered the book as historical. In fact, "the book presents itself as an historical account without any real indication that it should be interpreted otherwise" (*NCB* p. 781). "The fact that generations of scholars and writers were convinced that the author of Jonah did not intend to write fiction argues against the modern view that the form or style of the narrative conveys this very impression" (Alexander, "Jonah and Genre" p. 58).

The prophet Jonah is quoted in the abbreviated version of the book of Tobit (14:4). Ecclesiasticus (or The Wisdom of Sirach) refers to a dozen minor prophets: "As for the bones of these prophets, may they blossom again from their tomb, because they encouraged Jacob and they delivered him by faith and hope" (49:10). The prophet Jonah is thus considered to be a real person, and the author of the book which bears his name. Flavius Josephus (*Antiquities* 9.11 or 9.10.2) devotes two whole pages to Jonah and specifies that he cannot remain silent about this prophet, "Now I cannot but think it necessary for me, who have promised to give an accurate account of our affairs, to describe the actions of this prophet, so far as I have found them written down in the Hebrew books."

It is also fitting to mention that God is the key figure of the account. "Given Jewish attitudes concerning God, in particular the prohibitions against the making of idols and the improper use of the divine name, is it not highly improbable that a Jewish author of the period 780 to 350 BC would have dared create a fictional account with God as a central character? Would not this have been viewed by devout Jews of that time as tantamount to blasphemy?" (Alexander: "Jonah and Genre" p. 58). Thus the book of Jonah was not only included in the Hebrew canon, but it was never disputed, because no-one considered it to be a simple tale. It is in fifth place on the scroll of the dozen minor prophets, and thus located amongst the prophets of the 9th and 8th centuries.[13]

Jesus's Witness

The strongest evidence of Jonah's historicity comes from Jesus himself. He replies to the doubting scribes and Pharisees:

> *"... 'An evil and adulterous generation craves for a sign; and yet no sign will be given to it except the sign of Jonah the prophet; For just as Jonah was three days and three nights in the belly of a sea monster, so will the Son of Man be three days and three nights in the heart of the earth. The men of Nineveh will stand up with this generation at the judgment, and will condemn it because they repented at the preaching of Jonah; and behold, something greater than Jonah is here. The Queen of the South will rise up with this generation at the judgment and will condemn it, because she came from the ends of the earth to hear the wisdom of Solomon; and behold, something greater than Solomon is here.'" (Mt 12:39-42)*

Jesus places the Ninevites' conversion and the queen of Sheba's visit to Solomon on the same level (cf. 1 Kings 10:1-13). Even more importantly, he makes a parallel between Jonah's time in the fish and his own death and resurrection. "Christ compares facts with facts, not fiction with fiction, or fiction with facts. It would certainly be very strange if he were to present himself as being greater than a fictional character; it would be equally odd for him to condemn the Jews for their lack of penitence by contrasting their deficiency with the repentance of a Nineveh which never existed." (Feuillet col. 1112). "The condemnation of Jesus' generation is far less effective if the repentance of the Ninevites is non-historical." (Bullock p. 46).

---

[13] Elmer Dyck: "Jonah among the Prophets: A Study in Canonical Context" in *JETS* 33/1 (1990) p. 63-73.

The Clues Left by the Author

The author provides an historical framework for his account. Not only is the prophet mentioned by name, but the book begins like historical accounts do (see Commentary, 1:1 p. 99). These first elements are very important, because they guide the course of the entire reading. "The reader's initial reaction to the text will determine how he continues to view the narrative. If the opening lines are stylistically in keeping with other historical narratives, it is only natural that he should treat the text as factual. However, if he begins by believing that these events took place, only to discover later, perhaps in Chapter 3, that this is pure fiction, he will feel misled, if not actually deceived and this is something which any competent author would clearly avoid."[14] Conversely, if an account begins with the expression "once upon a time...", the reader will immediately know that the account is not historical.

Having set the framework, the author concentrates on the essential elements of his account. Of course, his readers might like to have some other historical information (particularly a chronological reference, possibly the name of Nineveh's king), but the author sticks to a minimum, perhaps to show that his historical account goes beyond the borders of 8th-century history. The account of Jonah is historical, but it is also prophetic, as it announces the extent of God's grace beginning with the coming of the Messiah.

The Presence of Miracles

Modern man is often embarrassed by these miracles, and several commentators attempt to demythologize the accounts to make them acceptable and accessible to their contemporaries. Nevertheless, Biblical authors never had the slightest doubt about miracles. In fact, what is more natural than a Creator who intervenes in his creation? It was rather the absence of divine intervention that puzzled them.

---

[14] Alexander: In: "Jonah and Genre" p. 56-57.

In the book of Jonah, the miracles of the fish and of the Ninevites' repentance are exceptional, but the narrator does not lessen their impact. On the contrary, he mentions certain details which further accentuate the miracles. Jonah is not only saved by the fish, but he stays in the animal's stomach for *"three days and three nights."* The word "three" is repeated, and by mentioning "day" and "night" he seems to extend the length of time even further. The Ninevites' repentance is described from several angles: of the people, the nobility, the king, and the animals.

The miraculous dimension is mentioned, but the description of the wonders remains succint. We are far from Jewish tradition which imagines that the storm calmed down gradually, proportionately to the degree to which the prophet's body was immersed in the sea.[15] According to the same tradition, the prophet used the fish's eyes as portholes.[16] To justify the three days inside the fish, tradition also explains that God first had a male fish swallow Jonah. In view of the prophet's stubbornness and refusal to repent, God then had him spit out and inserted into a pregnant female fish. Caught in such tight quarters, Jonah finally submitted to the LORD.[17]

---

15 "First of all they asked him and then plunged him into the sea up to his knees, and the storm abated. But when they lifted him out of the water (to keep him from drowning), the sea became rough again. The second time, they held him in until the water was up to his navel, and the sea calmed, but as soon as they pulled him onto the deck, the sea began to stir up again. The third time around, they plunged him in up to his neck, and the same thing happened. (They felt that the three tests confirmed that Jonah was responsible [for the storm]). So they lifted Jonah up and threw him into the sea, and the sea raged no more." (Zlotowitz p. 103).

16 "The Sea of Reeds *was hanging over my head*. The eyes of the fish were like two windows through which Jonah could peer and contemplate the sea. Then, God showed Jonah the place where the sons of Israel crossed the Sea of Reeds" (Zlotowitz p. 113).

17 "Jonah had been swallowed by a male fish whose insides were relatively spacious and due to this fact, it did not occur to him to pray. God thus gave the fish a sign to spit Jonah into the mouth of a gestating female. Surrounded by hundreds of eggs, Jonah was in a tight situation

The miracle is confirmed, but it remains restrained and linked to creation. We are not in a supernatural world. God works with his creation, not outside of it. The elements used are the wind (westerly and easterly), large and small animals (fish and worm), a plant well-known in the region (the vine).

The defenders of historicity often strain to provide a rational explanation for the miracle of the fish and the Ninevites' mass repentance. Prior to presenting their arguments, it is necessary to mention that such a defense, no matter how interesting it might be, is not necessary. The narrator makes no such effort. For him, there is no discussion whatsoever of the LORD's sovereign act. The problem is not God's power in view of his creation; the trouble comes from man's difficulty to accept the extent of God's love.

The explanations of the fish are presented on the following pages and those regarding the Ninevites' repentance are explained in the Commentary in 3:6 (p. 139-142).

The Miracle of the Fish

Is it possible that a large fish could swallow a man alive? The particular species is not specified in the book of Jonah; the creature is merely described as a large "fish" (*daga*). The New Testament speaks of *kêtos* (Mt 12:40). It repeats the word used in the Greek translation of the Septuagint for the fish of Jonah (2:1, 11). The word *kêtos* led to the term "cetacean". Some older English translations, such as KJ, used the world *whale*, whilst modern translations have reverted to a more general term: "large fish".

The *whale* of Jonah is commonly used in the popular view, but commentators have often observed that this fish does not really fit the bill. According to *BA* (p. 125), "this animal cannot be a whale, because this cetacean does not exists in the Mediterranean, as well as the fact that its gullet is far too narrow to swallow a man." Other commentators support the contrary. "In 1956, a (dead) whale was

---

and that prompted him to pray." (Zlotowitz p. 108, see also Reichelberg p. 117).

purportedly found near the beach of Ascalon, south of Jaffa" (North p. 133). Gaebelein (p. 128) remarks that not all whales have the same throat form: "It has often been said that a whale has a throat so small that it would have difficulty swallowing an orange. The Greenland whale does indeed have a very small throat. But there are other whales which can swallow a man; in fact, some can engulf objects larger than a horse." In one theological publication[18], a university professor from Princeton showed that "Even a true whale could save a man from drowning if he managed to negotiate the air-supply tract of the mammal and reach the great laryngeal pouch." (Harrison p. 907; cf. Aalders p. 6).

The *sperm whale* (*Phyeter macrocephalus* or *catodon*) is more appropriate than a baleen whale. These cetaceans grow to a considerable size (up to 30 metres) and swallow large prey. "One was caught near the Azores; it contained a perfectly preserved, living squid in its stomach which was 10 m long and weighed 186 kg. The sperm whale was only 14.5 metres long. Larger specimens can handle an even greater catch." (Meier p. 51-52). Severals authors also mention the adventure of a sailor in 1891 who was swallowed by a sperm whale, then retrieved alive from the fish after it was harpooned and cut up.[19]

"*Killer whales* or *orcas*, which are 6 to 10 m long, also swallow large prey: dolphins, narwals, sea bass and seals." (Meier p. 51). They were still present in the Mediterranean during the Middle Ages

Certain species of *shark* are also a possibility. "Since Bochart, the general opinion is that the fish had to be a type of shark, *Lamia canis carcharias*. Entire human bodies have been found inside these monsters, and we could even quote some recent examples of persons who have been recovered alive from them." (*NDB* p. 691). A famous case occurred in 1758, when a sailor who had fallen into the sea was swallowed by a shark, then spit back out when the captain

---

[18] G. Macloskie "How to Test the Story of Jonah" in *Bibliotheca Sacra* 72 (1915) p. 336ss.

[19] Gaebelein p. 129; Archer, *A Survey of Old Testament*, p. 302 footnote 8; Exell p. xii; Harrison p. 907.

shot a harpoon at the beast. According to the captain's testimony, the sailor toured Europe and exhibited the fish.[20]

Rabbinical commentaries assert the idea that the fish was specifically created by God when he created the world. "This fish was specially designated (i.e. chosen for this particular task) during the six days of creation to swallow Jonah. For this reason, he translates the phrase in the pluperfect (the LORD had designated 1:17)" (Zlotowitz p. 104-105). However, the spoken form of the verb *manâh* (to designate, to summon) is the same as in 4:6, 7, and 8 where the action describes God's intervention by means of the vine, the worm and the wind. The book of Jonah teaches that God uses ordinary "objects" of his creation to carry out his plans.

In conclusion, the identity of the fish remains uncertain, but God could have used more than one existing species to save Jonah.

The Literary Genre

The account of Jonah contains a number of astounding elements (which we have already mentioned in the first chapter, p. 13-19). However, these alone are insufficient reasons to classify the book as a parable. The parable genre is applicable to several different types of account, which nevertheless all contain common characteristics. Parables are brief, simple, applicable to a precise situation, and are accompanied by an interpretation if the meaning is difficult; they do not contain miracles or proper names,[21] and are not related to a true story. The account of Jonah does not fulfil any of these characteristics. It is long[22] and complex (Jonah's

---

[20] Gaebelein p. 129. See also Archer, *A Survey of Old Testament Introduction*, p. 302 footnote 8; *BA* p. 125; *Princeton Theological Review* Oct. 1927.

[21] The story of the rich man and poor Lazarus (Lk 16:19-31) may be the exception which confirms the rule (see Kuen p.425-426). We note, however, that Luke does not identify the account as a parable.

[22] The longest of Jesus's parables are less than half as brief as Jonah: the prodigal son (22 verses: Lk 15:11-32), the sower (20 verses: Mt 13:4-23), the talents (17 verses: Mt 25:14-30), the workers hired at different hours (16 verses: Mt 20:1-16). The average length of Jesus's parables

behaviour changes incessantly); there is no general explanation (the account raises many questions which remain unanswered); it is full of miracles, and the main character can be identified with a prophet who is well known to the readers.

Feuillet (col. 1111) also observes that "in ancient times, people were generally not in the habit of creating pure fiction which had no link to real events." In fact, "the strength of most of the Biblical parables resides precisely in their seeming resemblance to a real human situation." (*NCB* p. 780).

Several authors point out the narrator's use of irony or satire to negate the events' historicity. Yet these literary characteristics are not restricted to works of fiction. "The satirical character of the narration is dangerously invoked as proof of a non-historical genre. There are exquisite satires which report a selection of details which actually happened ." (North p. 136).

In the same way, an account's elaborate structure does not prove the non-historicity of the events described. "The presence of such poetic features does not in itself necessarily contradict the book's facticity. As D. Alexander correctly observes: 'The fact that the author of Jonah employs particular literary devices tells us more about his skill as an author than about the historicity or non-historicity of his account... There is no reason why a skillful author could not use there (literary structures and patterns) and still present an accurate account of what took place'"[23]

As to the typology, it always seems to be based on historical events. "Each time Scripture mentions a 'typological' event (for example Jn 3:14; 1 Co 10:1-11), it is a historical event."[24] "Only fiction can correspond to fiction; only fact can correspond to fact. All other types of Christ in the Old Testament were historical (Isaac's near sacrifice on

---

is six times shorter than Jonah (8 verses as opposed to 48). In the Old Testament, Jotham's parable (Jug 9:8-15) is composed of 8 verses, and that of Nathan has 4 verses (2 Sa 12:1-4).

23 Ernst R. Wendland: "Text Analysis and the Genre of Jonah, part 2" p. 387.

24 Archer, *A Survey of Old Testament Introduction*, p. 301

Mount Moriah, the priest-king Melchizedek, Moses, David, Solomon as types of Christ), as were the Exodus events referred to in 1 Corinthians 10 in a series of types and examples for believers in Paul's day"[25]

For some commentators, the improbability of events is a stumbling block for their historicity. But what is improbable for us was not necessarily so in earlier times (Alexander, "Jonah and Genre" p. 45); the first readers could very well have considered this text as historical. If the author presents his work as being historical, do we have the right to put it in a different category? Other critics emphasize the narrator's exaggerations to contest the account's historicity. They draw attention to the repeated use of the word "large". But Alexander points out that the word "large" is not used in an exaggerated fashion when referring to the city, the wind blowing on the sea, the sailors' fear or the fish. Furthermore, the miracles are described quite straightforwardly, without embellishment.

The Problems Which Arise with a Post-Exile Framework

To state that the account of Jonah is a polemic story written after the exile to counter Ezra's and Nehemiah's nationalistic politics causes a number of problems. The most obvious is linked to the destruction of Nineveh in 612 B.C. Who would want to write a story about God's universal grace by choosing a city which no longer existed? The account would no longer be credible, even more so because Nahum had already announced its fall several decades earlier. The great pardon of God would be shattered into pieces. The author of such a story would have chosen a large city of his own times, like Damascus or Tyre, to encourage universality.[26]

---

25 Archer, *Encyclopedia of Bible Difficulties*, p. 302.

26 "The account would not have meant anything anymore after the destruction of Nineveh in 612 B.C... 'Should I not be concerned about that great city?' would not only be a hypothetical remark, but one of extremely bad taste." (*NCB* p. 781). Some authors remark that Nineveh

The choice of Jonah as a "nationalistic" prophet is also not necessarily evident. In fact, "The reference to Jonah in 2 Kings 14:25 does not portray him as a zealous Israelite nationalist, as commentators who hold the anti-exclusivist approach claim. The text merely states that Jonah correctly prophesizes an expansion of Israel's borders; it does not say how Jonah feels or thinks about his prophecy, this particular turn of events, or any other matter." (Bolin p. 59). Furthermore, the text of 2 Kings 14:26 underscores the LORD's compassion towards Israel and not God's judgment of a domineering people. See also footnote 11 p. 29.

As to the "universalist" movement amongst the Jews of Ezra's and Nehemiah's time, it seems to have had more of a materialistic character rather than a missionary one. Maintaining harmonious relations with pagan neighbours was considered necessary to maintain and develop commercial exchanges.

The supposed irony against Jonah in the book also poses a problem. Although Feuillet (col. 1111) feels that "it is difficult to conceive that Jonah would have written such a biting and ironic critique of his own character", he admits something that is even more improbable in our view: "A previous writer would not have dared to attack the memory of this prophet by attributing such narrow-mindedness to him." Why tarnish a man of God from the past? And above all, how could anyone imagine that a polemic treatise which scorns a prophet to such a degree would be accepted into the canon? In addition, what Jew would be convinced of God's universalism by a simple story?

---

is described in 'perfect' Hebrew (*hayethath*) in 3:3: "Nineveh *was* a very important city", which would prove that the city no longer existed at the time the book was written. Archer (*A Survey of Old Testament Introduction*, p. 298) states: "It is readily conceded that the author might well have expressed the size of Nineveh by use of the imperfect tense (*tiheyeh*) had he chosen to do so; but it was evidently his particular purpose at that point in the narrative to stress the fact that Nineveh had already become a very sizable city (though it had probable become even larger by the time the book was written, that is, in 760 B.C.). The only way to express this thought, 'had become', was by the use of the perfect tense, *hayetah*."

Finally, we would like to emphasize that the allegorical message is far from clear. If the fish symbolizes Babylon, what does Nineveh represent? And why mention a stay of "three days" inside the fish, rather than seven, for example, to represent the seventy years of captivity?

The Historical Context of the 8th Century

The historical context of Jonah is set by a verse in the book of Kings: *"He (Jeroboam II) restored the border of Israel from the entrance of Hamath as far as the Sea of the Arabah, according to the word of the LORD, the God of Israel, which He spoke through His servant Jonah the son of Amittai, the prophet, who was of Gath-hepher."* (2 Kings 14:25). Jonah thus prophesied in Israel's favour before or during the reign of Jeroboam II, who was king of Israel for 40 years (2 Kings 14:23), from 793 to 753 B.C. Theoretically, the prophet's ministry at Nineveh could also have taken place after the death of Jeroboam II, which would leave a period of a century for the voyage to Nineveh (approximately from 830 to 720). Nevertheless, the exegetes feel that Jonah announced the restoration of Israel's borders at the start of Jeroboam's reign; because that king had a prosperous reign on the material level; he must have swiftly subdued the Syrians who were threatening him from the northeast.

This period and several decades before are also characterized by intern dissent amongst Assyrians. This might explain the Ninevites' great receptivity to Jonah's message of repentance.[27]

The Assyrians' cruelty was well known and lasted for several centuries. H. R. Hall gives us a detailed description of the Assyrian king Ashur-nasir-pal II (883-859): "His usual procedure after the capture of a hostile city was to burn it, and then to mutilate all the grown male prisoners by cutting off their hands and ears and putting out their eyes; after which they were piled up in a great heap to perish in torture from sun, flies, their wounds and suffocation; the children, both boys and girls, were all burnt alive at the stake; and the

[27] See Commentary, 3:5-6: footnote 16 p. 123 and point 3 p. 125.

chief was carried off to Assyria to be flayed alive for the king's delectation"[28]

An Assyrian invasion of Palestine can be dated at 805 B.C.E., a period which would correspond with Jonah's childhood. According to Wiseman (p. 50) and Baldwin (p. 545), "Adad-nerari III (810-783) has left a firsthand description of his expedition to Pa-la-as-tu (Palestine) in the fifth year of his reign (ANET, pp. 281-82), when 'according to the Rimah stela, (he) exacted recognition from Ia'usa (Joash) of Samaria' (Wiseman 'Jonah's Nineveh' p. 50)". This invasion could have affected Jonah and left traces of bitterness.

Supposed Historical Errors and Aramaic Terms

Replies to supposed historical errors are developed in the commentary. The following are defended: the king of Nineveh's authenticity (p. 142-143), the three days' march through Nineveh (p. 135-137) and the city's 120,000 inhabitants (p. 162).

The presence of Aramaic terms in the Hebrew text does not imply a post-exile writing of the book.[29] To begin with, this concerns only very few words: *sailors* (1:5), *ship* (1:5), *decree* (3:7), *proclamation* (3:2), *take notice* (1:6). The last two on the list are hapax, i.e. rare terms which are not characteristic for the setting. The first three terms are linked to Jonah's time abroad (sailors, ship, decree). What traveller does not return from a vacation abroad bearing some 'exotic' words in tow? Next, a more general critique consists of comparing the book of Jonah with other books of the Bible and ascertaining that the presence of arameisms is not

[28] H.R.Hall, *The Ancient History of the Near East*, p. 445, quoted by Jensen p. 27 and by H.L. Ellison, *The Prophets of Israel*, p. 57.

[29] Detailed refutations have been made by different authors: Aalders, *The Problem of the Book of Jonah*, p. 11-12; Archer, *A Survey of Old Testament Introduction*, p. 300-301; Bolin p. 37; Ermoni, *Dictionnaire Catholique Vigouroux*, col. 1607; Alexander, *Tyndale OT Commentaries*, p. 52-55.

restricted to the post-exile books. "The presence of arameisms in the book cannot be considered as a criterion for its date, because arameisms are found in the books of the Old Testament of the first and last period."[30] "One finds proof of arameisms in very primitive periods."[31] The proximity of the two languages goes back to ancient times.

The Fundamental Importance of Historicity

The defense of the Biblical account's historicity is important, but it must not be undertaken to the detriment of the Bible message's analysis. Unfortunately, this is not always the case. "In expending so much time defending and even trying to prove that the amazing and miraculous events of the book actually happened, most conservatives have missed the tremendous theological and practical insights that many liberals have proposed from their critical studies." In other words, "Men have been looking so hard at the great fish that they have failed to see the great God".[32]

Nevertheless, the defense of Jonah's historicity remains an important task, because to reject it often leads to the rejection of other historical accounts.[33] Jonah is on the front line of liberal attacks, and is often one of the first accounts to be trapped in a historical criticism. A game of dominoes follows. Once Jonah is rejected, the critics attack other accounts of miracles, beginning with the most spectacular ones, like those of Elijah and Elisha, which are inserted in a historical book (1-2 Kings). Once they have entered the vicious circle of autonomous critique, the commentators have difficulty

---

30 *NCB* p. 781 who quotes E. J. Young, *Introduction to the Old Testament*, 1953, p. 255.

31 *NCB* p. 781 who quotes Morris, 'Ruth', 1968.

32 Allen p. 192 who quotes G. Campbell Morgan: *The Minor Prophets*, 1960, p. 69. Feinberg (p. 137) goes in the same direction when he states: "The character and dimensions of the fish are of secondary importance to us. More important than the fish is the man!"

33 See Aalders p. 15-19.

stopping, and some even go so far as to reject the fundamental events surrounding the life of Christ.[34]

The defense of Jonah's historicity serves not only as a barrier against a liberal drift; it also protects the very message of the book. In the book of Jonah, The LORD reveals himself as the God who does his utmost to save men. All of creation is involved. The LORD uses all of his resources to transmit salvation to the Ninevites. This gigantic deployment of divine resources announces the coming of Jesus Christ. Then, more than in Jonah's day, God did all he could to save mankind. He was incarnated in the person of Jesus Christ, who died on the cross. Is it really possible that God loved man so much that he went so far as to give his only Son so that anyone who would believe in him would be saved? (cf. Jn 3:16). If the book of Jonah were only a fable, that would mean that God did not have such an effect on the history of that time as the book proposes. It would mean that the book of Jonah does not really announce the ministry of redemption fulfilled in Jesus Christ.[35] The historicity of Jonah does not merely serve as a biodegradable packaging for the message; it is its spinal column.[36] Without historicity, there is no message. We would fall from the marvellous reality of God's love into the desperate utopia of our dreams.

---

[34] For the liberal A.K.M. Adam ("The Sign of Jonah: A Fish-Eye View", p. 186), the determination of the literary genre and the rejection of Jonah's historicity "makes all the difference in the world": "If Jonah is fictional, and Jesus was not prescient, readers simply cannot seriously propose the interpretations which seemed obvious in the first century."

[35] Ellul (p. 2) is obviously completely mistaken with his criticism of the defenders of historicity: "To vehemently confirm, against all reason, that the book of Jonah is the materially exact history of the facts which took place in that way does not appear to me to be a particularly Christian attitude, because it definitively leads us away from the book's true reality which is Christ."

[36] We note in passing that the Hebrew text was very well preserved and contains very few variants (Allen p. 191-192; Wiseman "The text itself is virtually unquestioned, with few manuscript variants" p. 31; Alexander, *Tyndale OT Commentaries,* p. 96).

The Author of the Book

Jewish tradition attributes the book to Jonah, son of Amittai. "All of the ancient commentators considered Jonah as the prophet of the 8th century… not only as a hero, which is difficult to contest, but also as the author of our book" (Feuillet col. 1105). It must also be said that if the author had been a contemporary of the prophet, he would hardly have dared to ridicule him, and the same holds true for a later period. "It is more likely that this unflattering portrait is the work of a man who, having been taught an unforgettable lesson by a loving God, does not spare himself in setting it down, than that it is an imaginary story attached to the name of a prophet of a former age." (Gaebelein p. 59). This reasoning is certainly valid insofar as the prophet is being derided, which could be contested (see p. 20-21).

Some commentators have difficulty accepting Jonah as the author due to the absence of a final repentance. "In some ways, it would be natural for him (Jonah) more than any other, precisely because of the quite unpraisworthy role which he himself plays. Nevertheless, it is difficult to understand why there are no expressions of repentance at the end, following his almost insolent replies to the LORD." (*BA* p. 121). As we have already stated, the author does not mention any repentance in order to make the reader reflect better (see p. 19). At any rate, no narrator but Jonah would have known the information reported in the book without having a detailed testimony by Jonah himself. The prophet is well-hidden behind the book which bears his name, be it as its author, be it as a witness.

PART 2

COMMENTARY

CHAPTER 1

JONAH'S REVOLT

The LORD's Call: 1:1-2

> *1 The word of the LORD came to Jonah son of Amittai, saying: 2 "Arise, go to Nineveh the great city and cry against it, for their wickedness has come up before me."*

The account of Jonah begins in a classic manner: "*The word of the LORD came to Jonah son of Amittai.*" Four other prophets–Hosea, Joel, Micah, Zephania–start off their writings with the same elements: (1) the word (2) of the LORD (3) is addressed (4) to the prophet, (5) whose name is followed by the name of his father (or his origin Mi 1:1). This *classic* style of opening makes it possible to connect this *atypical* book to the other prophetic writings. Although very different from the canonical prophets, Jonah does not contradict them. He fits perfectly into the divine revelation given to mankind.

The book's first words also allow the immediate identification of the account's main character. The LORD is the silent partner of this new mission. He is also the one who watches over it so that it will take place properly. He is present from start to finish, because his words also end the book (4:10-11). The LORD is the account's main subject, and the book was written in order to make him better known. Obviously, the prophet Jonah also has an important place in it, and his enigmatic behaviour often leads the reader astray, to the point of monopolising his attention. But Jonah remains a secondary player. At the end of the line, his reactions to the LORD's orders enable us to know the LORD better.

At first, the LORD is presented as the just and holy God who hates sin. God's patience has its limits, and when men unceasingly scoff at his law, God must intervene. This aspect of God's person is familiar to Israelite readers. The author thus departs from this experience to lead his contemporaries onto a new path, at any rate towards a lesser known aspect of the LORD (cf. 4:2).

The expression *"its wickedness has come up before me"* is reminiscent of the one used for Sodom and Gomorrah: *"Then the LORD said, 'The outcry of Sodom and Gomorrah is indeed great, and their sin exceedingly grave. I will go down now, and see if they have done entirely according to its outcry, which has come to me; and if not, I will know.'"* (Ge 18:20-21). The reader would feel as though he were faced with a new Sodom and Gomorrah story: God ready to destroy another flourishing pagan city corrupted by sin.[1] In fact, in a general manner, both Nineveh and the Assyrians were known for their cruelty. Frescoes discovered at Nineveh depict the different kinds of torture inflicted upon the cities who refused Assyrian domination; their inhabitants were quartered and impaled.[2]

However, a comparison between Nineveh and the two patriarchal cities of the Jordan valley can only be partial. In Sodom and Gomorrah's case, God had informed Abraham of the cities' imminent destruction without giving the patriarch a mandate for any specific mission. Jonah, on the other hand, was to go and announce judgment to Nineveh (see Parallels p. 56-58).

Jonah's mission is unique in the Bible. Never had a prophet been asked to announce such a message to a *foreign* people. Indeed, Hebrew prophets often announced judgments upon Israel and Judah to their compatriots. Prophets sometimes spoke judgment upon pagan nations–Isaiah (Is 13-

---

1 "Though Nineveh was the largest city of Assyria at this time, it was not the capital city" (Wood p. 290). It became the capital during the reign of Sennacherib, more than half a century after Jonah's visit.

2 "The Assyrians were well known for the brutal atrocities they inflicted on their war captives (impaling survivors on stakes in front of their towns; erecting pillars of skulls from slain warriors; nobles/chief officials hanging heads around their necks to demonstrate the power of their god Asshur)" Schrader p. 645). See also p. 81.

23), Amos (Am 1), Nahum (Na 1-3), Jeremiah (Jer 46-51), Ezekiel (Ez 25-32)–but their message was always directed towards their Hebrew compatriots, the messages of destruction serving to encourage the chosen people to be patient when faced with the temporary success of enemy nations.

Why did God choose to give such a mandate to a prophet for such a special mission? Commentators unfortunately often sidestep this vital question. Before replying (in our analysis of verse 3), we must first deal with the messenger's identity.

The prophet is identified by name and with the name of his father: *"Jonah, son of Amittai"*. It is not much, but enough for the Israelites to situate him. In fact, the Old Testament mentions the prophet only once outside of the book of Jonah. In 2 Kings 14:25, it is said that Jeroboam, king of Israel, *"...restored the border of Israel from the entrance of Hamath as far as the Sea of the Arabah, according to the word of the LORD, the God of Israel, which he spoke through his servant Jonah the son of Amittai, the prophet, who was of Gath Hepher."* Jonah thus comes from a place in the territory of Zebulon (cf. Jos 19:13)[3], within the kingdom of Israel. He is a contemporary of Jeroboam II, who reigned over Israel from 793 to 753 B.C. (see Historical Context p. 91-92).

The meaning of the two proper names is important. *Jonah* means "dove" and *Amitai* means "truth". Jonah is literally "the dove of truth". The dove symbolises both peace and pardon, as well as judgment because of its unpleasant cry.[4] Thus, Jonah incarnates judgment and grace at the same time,

---

3 Gath-Hepher is located five kilometres northeast of Nazareth.

4 "The dove (*yonah*) is known for its plaintive cry (Es 38:14; 59:11); for its stupidity (Hos 7:11); for its powerful flight (Ps 55:7); for its fidelity to its companion and its tenderness (So 2:14; 5:2; 6:9). In general, this ritually pure animal is mentioned with affection. In many cases, it is a metaphor for the people of Israel (Ps 68:14; 74:19; Hos 7:11; 11:11)" (Lacocque p. 46). The New Testament mentions the dove in connection with the Spirit coming upon Jesus at his baptism (Mt 3:16; Mk 1:10; Lk 3:22; Jn 1:32.)

because he must announce Nineveh's destruction, but in view of its salvation (cf. 4:2). The dimension of "truth" in Jonah is considered throughout the commentary. For the time being, we simply note that Jonah is a man known by his contemporaries as a prophet whose prophecy about the re-establishment of the borders came to pass (cf. 2 Kings 14:25), a man who gave out the word of the LORD correctly.

Jonah's Flight: 1:3

> *3 But Jonah rose up to flee to Tarshish from the presence of the LORD. So he went down to Joppa, found a ship which was going to Tarshish, paid the fare and went down into it to go with them to Tarshish from the presence of the LORD.*

Jonah completely rejects God's call. Instead of undertaking a voyage by land 1000 kilometres east of Israel to go to Nineveh, Jonah takes a ship to Tarshish, located 3800 kilometres west of Israel.[5] Everything is said in one sentence: *"But Jonah rose up to flee to Tarshish from the presence of the LORD"*. These words express the meaning of the procedure: fleeing from the LORD, in other words resisting divine will with all one's might.

Disconcerted by Jonah's reaction, the reader asks himself what the reasons for the rejection of the divine mission could

---

[5] "Many scholars favour the identification of Tarshish with Tartessos, a Phoenician colony on the Atlantic coast of southern Spain at the mouth of the river Guadalquivir. Apart from the similarity in names, two factors favour this identification. Firstly, several biblical references associate Tarshish with distant places (Ps. 72:10; Is 66:19). The same impression is given by a short comment in a cuneiform inscription of the Assyrian king Esarhaddon (680-669 BC): 'All kings who live in the midst of the sea, from Cyprus and Javan as far as Tarshish, submit to my feet'. Secondly, Tarshish was renowned as a source of silver, iron, tin and lead (Je. 10:9; Ezk. 27:12), and, significantly, after 1000 BC one of the most important sources of these metals in the ancient world was the Iberian peninsula." (Alexander, *Tyndale OT Commentaries*, p. 100). Other locations have been proposed, but commentators disagree on them: (1) Tarsus in Cilicia, (2) Carthage in North Africa, (3) south of Cagliari in Sardinia (North p. 129).

be. Why refuse the call? Why flee in the opposite direction? These questions are as fundamental as those which concern the mission's goal. Yet the narrator provides no immediate answer; he merely repeats the key elements of the different steps and adds a few details about the voyage itself: place of embarkment[6], search for a ship, cost of the journey[7]. These details underscore the prophet's determination–he is prepared to spend all of his money and rub shoulders with pagans (passengers and crew members lived closely together on board)–to carry out his project.[8]

---

6 Jaffa was the only port of any importance on the Palestinian coast at that time (*NCB* p. 782). "Ironically, the city Jonah visited to escape his mission to the Gentiles was the city where Peter's vision would mark the beginning of the mission to the Gentiles in the New Covenant (Acts 10:9-23)" (Kohlenberger p. 30). Peter was to go to Caesarea Maritima afterwards, the great port on the Palestinian shore during Roman times, from whence travellers went to Rome and to the outer limits of the Mediterranean. We would also like to point out Peter is "Simon, the son of *Jonah*", and that this detail is given in three Scripture passages which emphasize the apostle's missionary and pastoral mandate (Mt 16:17-18; Jn 1:42; 21:15-17)! This may be more than just a coincidence. Jesus voluntarily mentions Peter's father (Jonah) in order to include Peter's ministry in the line of the prophet of the same name.

7 *"After paying the fare, he went aboard and sailed"(NIV)* Why does the narrator mention this detail and which sum did Jonah pay? "It has been estimated that their journey via many ports of call could have taken as long as a year, so when Jonah paid his fare he is likely to have parted with a considerable sum of money." (Baldwin p. 553). Jewish commentators suggest that "Jonah was in such a hurry to board that he paid for all of the available places on the ship" (Zlotowitz p. 84-85), because a ship did not leave shore before a sufficient number of passengers had been assembled in order to fill all of the berths. "The term *sekara* indicates that he paid his price (to her), the rental of the ship, as the word '*oniya*, ship, is feminine) and not simply 'a seat' or 'his seat'. He paid prior to embarking on the ship, which is important, as passengers generally did not pay until after disembarking." (Zlotowitz p. 85).

8 Some translations indicate in verse 3 that the passengers were on board with the prophet (Seg, Col, NEG: *"Jonah embarked for Tarshish with the passengers"*). Other versions mention the crew (TOB, Sem, FC, Good News Bible: *"Jonah paid his fare and went abroad with the crew to sail to Spain")*. The Hebrew text provides no precise details on the identities of the individuals who accompanied the prophet; it simply

The narrator wants to make the reader ponder and to do so, he avoids revealing clues too quickly. An answer discovered after much seeking sticks in the mind more firmly than a reply provided without any reflection. In the Commentary, we have opted for the opposite procedure for reasons of clarity. To explain the enigmatic reactions of Jonah and the LORD, we felt it was more judicious to answer the book of Jonah's three fundamental questions at the start of the Commentary. These questions concern the reason for his refusal, the reason for his flight and the meaning of his unique mission.

1. Refusal of the mission. Jonah is not the only prophet to have refused a divine mission. Moses (Ex 3:7-4:17), Gideon (Jug 6:11-24), Jeremiah (Jer 1:6) and others cringed at the thought of following the LORD's call. After more or less well formulated objections by the elected and more or less convincing responses from the LORD, these men nevertheless all ended up submitting themselves to the LORD, just like Jonah.[9] Moses, Gideon and Jeremiah did not feel qualified for the task assigned to them by God and they feared opposition from their contemporaries. This kind of reason immediately comes to mind in Jonah's case. Who would be brave enough to announce the LORD's imminent judgment to a bloodthirsty people?

To assess the danger which awaited Jonah, it suffices to think of the two angels sent to Sodom to save Lot. Had they not immediately been hounded by the men of the city, although they had not uttered one single word of condemnation? They were only able to escape unscathed because of their supernatural powers (Ge 19:4-11). Fear seems to be a perfect explanation for Jonah's refusal, but the continuation of the account invalidates this

---

says *to go with "them"* (Dar, Jér, KJ, NIV, LB). Because the account makes no reference to passengers other than Jonah, it is preferable not to introduce them here. This makes it easier to understand why God's wrath threatened all of the human beings on board (see Commentary on v.12).

[9] The book of Kings reports the dramatic fate of two prophets who clearly disobeyed the LORD (1 Kings 13:1-32; 20:35-36).

explanation. In fact, Jonah himself confesses near the end of the book that the profound reason for his refusal is linked to the LORD and not to the Ninevites (4:2). Jonah refused to go to Nineveh for fear that the LORD would pardon the Ninevites and postpone his judgment.[10]

2. Flight to Tarshish. The narrator never gives any explanation of the reasons for Jonah's flight other than that the prophet wishes to *"flee... from the LORD"*. But how are these words to be interpreted? Did Jonah think it was possible to reach a place on earth where the LORD was inactive, or even powerless? Such an explanation clashes with Jonah's very confession in the middle of the sea at the height of the storm, where he confirms that he is the servant of God, Creator of the heavens, the sea and the land (1:9). Moreover, Jonah is so convinced of the LORD's power and his sway over all creation that he announces that the tempest will stop if he is thrown

---

[10] Nevertheless, Jonah could have feared the Ninevites, because even though he sensed their repentance in advance, he had no assurance of it. His mission to Nineveh was risky, but that was not the reason for his flight. Jonah is thus a courageous man because he finally does go to Nineveh (see p. 24).

Other reasons have been proposed to explain Jonah's refusal. (1) According to Jewish tradition, Nineveh was the capital of Assyria, which was not yet a great power at that time. This pagan nation could have easily been motivated to repent. If the Ninevites did indeed repent, they might then have pointed an accusing finger at Jerusalem who rejected all appeals for repentance. "If Jonah went to Nineveh, he would become the instrument of a condemnation without appeal for Israel. Jonah was faced with a tragic choice: obey God or save Israel's honour. To spare the child from the Father's rod, he decides not to go to Nineveh." (Scherman p. xxviii). (2) Jonah could also have been motivated by the Ninevites' hate or by fear of the suffering which this people could inflict upon Israel. The survival of such a bloodthirsty nation would have only meant trouble for Israel. (3) If the count down against Nineveh had started as soon as Jonah had heard the message, the prophet might hope to decrease the time of grace by going in the opposite direction. See also point 2, p. 22.

overboard, a prophecy which is fulfilled as soon as the this condition is carried out (1:15).[11]

It would be preferable to think that Jonah expresses *a non-verbal opposition to God* with his flight. Actions speak louder than words. Children, students, employees often show their opposition to power silently. Instead of objecting verbally, a child can pout or roll its eyes upward as a sign of contempt, spite or grief. It can turn around, slam the door, run away. The most extreme reaction, suicide (or attempted suicide) is often used to get attention and blame family members or society.

By leaving the Promised Land and fleeing to Tarshish, Jonah turns his back on the LORD and expresses his profound disagreement with him. Jonah does not just refuse the divine mission, because to do that he could have stayed in Israel. Jonah insists on *expressing* his disagreement in the strongest possible terms. He is prepared to leave his friends, his native land, the Promised Land. He is ready to empty his pockets and live amongst pagans to let the LORD know how much this divine project upsets him.

3. His special mission. To understand Jonah's displeasure, we must grasp the special meaning of his mission. Jonah must not simply give sinners an opportunity to repent. Jonah's mission is unique. If God decides to offer the Ninevites a chance of salvation, at this very precise moment of human history, and by sending a Hebrew prophet to announce God's word, it is because God wants to give a sign, to his prophet and by his prophet, of the extent of his love for mankind. It is the type of landmark which will indicate the geographical

---

11 A Jewish commentary proposes the following explanation: "On board a ship, Jonah hoped to avoid another prophetic call, either because he imagined that a ship's passengers are so anxious about their safety until they are back on shore again (and prophetic visions can only be received by a person whose spirit is completely calm), or because if he was on a ship crammed with and surrounded by pagans, he would not be in the condition required for a prophetic communication." (Zlotowitz p. 83).

extent of grace and the depth of the pardon. Nineveh was chosen because it was one of the well-known cities which was furthest away from Israel and because it had a reputation of extreme cruelty. Jonah being a prophet, his mission is thus prophetic, and it is the main purpose of his mission. The mission is a declaration of the LORD's intention to extend his love and grace to all men on the face of the earth at a time of his choosing, no matter what their state of moral or spiritual degeneration might be. Jonah's mission is fundamentally Christ-centred.

Jonah understands the meaning of the mission and the message which God wishes to pass on through this prophetic gesture, as he states in Chapter 4: *"I knew that you are a gracious and compassionate God, slow to anger and abundant in lovingkindness, and one who relents concerning calamity."* (4:2). Thus, Jonah contests the fact that God extends his love to all men, even to the worst evildoer. Is he jealous of his own people (cf. Ro 11:11)? Is it due to a sense of justice? Does he think that an unduly generous pardon will lead the people to total depravity (cf. Ro 6:1)? There can be many different reasons.

The LORD's Reaction: 1:4

> *4 The LORD hurled a great wind on the sea and there was a great storm on the sea so that the ship was about to break up.*

God uses impressive means to reply to Jonah's vigorous contention. A wrestling match begins between the LORD and his prophet. God puts himself on his rival's terrain and also expresses himself in a non-verbal manner. Jonah has chosen to flee to the other end of the world to mark his disagreement. God chooses to signal His disapproval by hindering Jonah from carrying out his project. Wind and tempest are wielded against Jonah. The divine message is clear to the prophet, because he later recognizes that the celestial elements have been unleashed *against him* (1:12).

The LORD's response is strong and it seems disproportionate, just as Jonah's reaction is intense and also seems overdone. God is prepared to drown his prophet and at the same time let the crew of a huge ship (as well as possible passen Several gers) perish to punish his chosen one for not carrying out a mission which is meant to testify God's compassion for all men! God's ways seem so unfathomable! But God is not a hothead who reacts to men's actions without reflection. The following pages will allow us to comprehend the coherence of God's reaction. For now, we note that the shipwreck does not happen immediately. God displays his anger, but he gives men time to react. God's "method" is identical to the one he plans for the Ninevites. A judgment of destruction is announced, but at the same time a period of grace is granted: *"Yet forty days and Nineveh will be overthrown"* (3:4).

Jonah's and the Pagans' Reactions: 1:5

> *5 Then the sailors became afraid and every man cried out to his god, and they threw the cargo which was in the ship into the sea to lighten it for them. But Jonah had gone below into the hold of the ship, lain down and fallen sound asleep.*

The pagans use the time of grace to save themselves. They make every attempt to stay alive. All possible means of salvation are applied simultaneously; no solution is omitted. Each person invokes his gods and the ship is divested of all superfluous objects. Even the loss of the cargo is accepted in the hope of survival.

Jonah's reaction is completely opposite to that of the sailors. He is not the slightest bit active, he says no prayer, he is totally passive. He descends to the hold, lies down and falls *into a deep sleep*[12]. What is the explanation for this behaviour?

---

[12] The verb *râdam* (sleep) is used only seven times in the Old Testament. It implies a profound slumber (Jug 4:21; Pr 10:5) or an unconscious state (Da 8:18; 10:9). The Septuagint translation states that Jonah "fell asleep and snored". *NCB* (p. 783): "The LXX adds the detail that it was Jonah's snoring as he lay asleep in the sides of the ship that first attracted the shipmaster's attention to the suspicious traveller."

Is Jonah physically tired, unconscious, out of his senses, suicidal, or, on the contrary, full of faith? He chooses the most vulnerable spot at the very bottom of the ship, and prostrates himself on the planks where the water will gather first when the ship is flooded.

According to certain commentators, his sleep is due to the fatigue of the voyage and Jonah's frantic efforts to find a ship bound for Tarshish. Once he was at sea, he would have been exhausted and weary. Sleep is also a way to make time pass more quickly, particularly on a long voyage. Others think that it was exhaustion caused by stress and a bad conscience. But why does the narrator, who has previously been very succinct, tell this anecdote? Furthermore, sleep is mentioned after the storm. Jonah would thus not have laid himself to sleep at the start of the voyage, but only after the tempest had started.

Did Jonah seek refuge in sleep because of the danger of the storm or for fear of God's judgment? A lethargic state would prevent him from reflecting and from having to face divine wrath.[13] Was the prophet suicidal, and had he lost his lust for life? Does he not suggest to the sailors later on that they should throw him into the sea (v. 12)? That type of explanation, however, conflicts with the prayer of deliverance he addresses to the LORD amongst the waves (2:2). Jonah obviously wants to stay alive—unless he is so unstable that he wants to live at one moment and wishes to die at the next instant.

Is it possible to view Jonah's behaviour as a sign of his confidence in the LORD? Didn't Jesus also sleep in a boat during a storm on the lake of Galilee because of his confidence in his heavenly Father (Mt 8:23-27)? But Jesus was in full communion with his Father, whereas Jonah is in a state of rebellion. The LORD's peace is granted only to the faithful.

One last explanation consists of viewing Jonah's procedure as a sign of non-verbal contention towards the

---

13 According to *BA* (p. 124), the prophet down in the ship's hold "had fled the light and sought both to forget his error in the depths of slumber as well as rest for his troubled conscience."

LORD. Descending to the hold, the most dangerous spot for a nap in the midst of a fierce storm, is a way of ignoring the LORD's non-verbal message. The wrestling match between the LORD and his prophet continues. Jonah does not waver in face of the death threat. He continues to oppose the LORD. In the beginning, he had turned his back on him by fleeing to Tarshish. Now he turns a deaf ear to him, he closes his eyes and refuses to see the storm. This attitude is the height of arrogance. When a child acts like that towards its parent, the latter must control himself to avoid exploding with anger.

It must be said that children often test the limits of parental anger with their protest, and try to see how far they can go without suffering any injury. Protesting minorities do the same. How far does an authority threaten its subjects? Yet Jonah knows the LORD God very well. He knows he is *"a gracious and compassionate God, slow to anger and abundant in lovingkindness, and one who relents concerning calamity"* (4:2). With the LORD, judgment is not immediate; it is generally deferred. Jonah thus ignores the LORD's request. He insists on objecting. Does Jonah believe that God will keep him alive against all odds, because of his mission's importance? Probably not, because no-one is indispensable to God, and Jonah knows his LORD too well to even consider such a thought. The LORD does not ignore sin. He is not a God who never punishes evil, but Jonah probably feels that his contention does not deserve death.

The Pagans Pursue Their Efforts of Salvation: 1:6-8

6 The captain approached him and said, "How is it that you are sleeping? Get up, call on your god. Perhaps your god will be concerned about us so that we will not perish." 7Each man said to his mate, "Come, let us cast lots so we may learn on whose account this calamity has struck us." So they cast lots and the lot fell on Jonah. 8Then they said to him, "Tell us, now! On whose account has this calamity struck us? What is your occupation? And where do you come from? What is your country? From what people are you?"

The pagans do not understand Jonah's odd behaviour. Everyone must join forces to keep the ship afloat. The captain asks the prophet about his passiveness, but because he receives no reply (or perhaps he doesn't give him time to answer, because at this point philosophical or religious reflections are the last thing on his mind), he gives him two orders: "Get up and pray." Action is vital to the captain.[14]

The narrator does not specify if Jonah obeys the pagan's injunctions, but everything leads us to believe that he does not. The captain, who appears to be caught up in the general frenzy—in stark contrast to Jonah who remains impassive—tries something else. He looks for someone to blame. *"Come, let us cast lots so we may learn on whose account this calamity has struck us."* This is a surprising procedure for an experienced sailor who has certainly gone through a number of storms at sea. Perhaps he is overwhelmed by the size of the storm (the narrator describes it as a *great* tempest). The captain may have possibly also discerned a supernatural cause.[15] Lots are immediately cast and, evidently steered by the LORD, they designate Jonah. As soon as the "guilty party" is identified, the captain bombards him with questions. The first one is surprising, because it concerns the identity of the person to blame for the disaster: *"Tell us, now! On whose account has this calamity struck us?"* Does the captain doubt that a man could be responsible for such a storm? The questions which tumble over the pagan's lips indicate a

---

14 Even if the answer to Jonah's behaviour is not essential for the captain, the narrator puts it into words, because it stimulates the reader's reflection about the question of why Jonah slept.

15 "Jewish tradition imagines a tempest which whirls the waters around Jonah's ship: Why should they presume that the storm's cause should be found on their own ship? Were they the only ones to cross the sea? Was it normal for ship's crews who were caught in a storm to cast lots to establish who was responsible? The storm in fact affected only Jonah's ship. The crew could see other ships to the right and left of them which sailed on unperturbedly on a perfectly calm sea." (Zlotowitz p. 92).

certain instability on his part. The man is helpless; he is overwhelmed by the events and cannot think clearly. The questions are all about his strange passenger: *"What is your occupation? And where do you come from? What is your country? From what people are you?"*[16]

Jonah's Answer: 1:9

> *9 He said to them, "I am a Hebrew, and I fear the LORD God of heaven who made the sea and the dry land."*

Several factors draw the reader's attention to Jonah's reply. (1) It is the first time that the narrator reports Jonah's words. Until now, the prophet's behaviour has been quite enigmatic. An explanation from him is thus most welcome. (2) Jonah's reply is preceded by an avalanche of questions related to his behaviour and identity (v. 8). Both the sailors and readers are waiting for an answer. (3) Jonah's reply is located structurally at the centre of the development (see p. 45).

But how is this answer to be understood? Jonah says that he *fears* the LORD, the creator God. Yet he is in complete rebellion against him. Can Jonah be taken seriously? Is he mocking, joking, being ironic? Has he lost his mind?

Jonah is not the type of person who would jest, certainly not under such circumstances. He is a serious, wholesome man who bears a heavy burden. His voyage to Tarshish costs him dearly–his money and his joy, because he has left the Promised Land with a heavy heart. Jonah is also a righteous man, "the son of truth". Even when confronted with the sailors' questions, he does not seek to conceal himself. He could have found any number of more or less coherent explanations to exonerate himself. Yet he does nothing of the kind, and even goes so far as to propose that he be thrown overboard (v. 12). Jonah speaks the truth.

---

16 *"What is your occupation?"* This is probably an unintentional play on words by the sailors. The word *melaka* has the same root as the word "messenger" (*malak*). And Jonah is a prophet (*nabi*), a messenger of God (Halpern p. 87).

The son of Amittai truly *fears* the LORD. The expression "fear the LORD" must be explained here: it means to have great respect for God. It does not mean to be terrified of him. Jonah has sufficient confidence in his God to contest him and to express his disagreement with him. God is certainly holy and sovereign, but he is also a God who respects humans. Each individual is important to him. It is possible to speak, discuss and even disagree with the God of the Bible—at least for a certain time—because God does not in advance reject the believer who asks him questions.[17] He leaves space for reflection, even if it takes the form of a contention as demonstrative as Jonah's.

Jonah is basically not a rebel. He is a man who loves the LORD, but also a man who has difficulty accepting one aspect of God's plan and who dares to say so. To understand the relationship between the LORD and Jonah better, one can consider the rough relationship which often exists between parents and adolescents. Despite differing opinions, it is important that the adolescent can express his reservations. Even if some words are hurtful for the parents, the dialogue itself is a sign of confidence.

The Pagans' Questions about the Solution: 1:10-11

> *10 Then the men became extremely frightened and they said to him, "How could you do this?" For the men knew that he was fleeing from the presence of the LORD, because he had told them. 11 So they said to him, "What should we do to you that the sea may become calm for us?"--for the sea was becoming increasingly stormy."*

The sailors are also afraid, but theirs is a different kind of fear because their relationship to the LORD is different. Their

[17] D. Arnold: "Peut-on questionner Dieu?" in *Promesses* 143 (2003) p. 3-5.

fear is *great*[18]; they are completely terrified. They cannot imagine that a man can contest the Creator, but the sailors know nothing of the God of the Covenant, this God who seeks companionship with men. For them, the Creator is only the Almighty. Anything which is contrary to his will can only be punished. Neither repentance nor pardon occur to them, only condemnation.

They ask Jonah rather naively about the punishment they must inflict upon him. Imagine a jury which asks a culprit to choose his own penalty! At any rate, this shows the sailors' confidence in Jonah's rectitude. The son of Amittai rebels against the LORD, but he is a righteous man who speaks the truth. They can believe his words.

Jonah's Solution: 1:12

> *12 "He said to them 'Pick me up and throw me into the sea. Then the sea will become calm for you, for I know that it is on account of me this great storm has come upon you."*

Why does Jonah ask the sailors to throw him into the sea? Does he share their thoughts that the punishment of the guilty party is the only thing which will satisfy the LORD? Is he depressed and suicidal, because in Chapter 4, he twice asks God to take his life (4:3, 8)? Or is he courageous and generous, prepared to sacrifice his life to save the sailors? But if the crew's salvation requires his sacrifice, why doesn't he throw himself into the sea? Is Jonah bluffing? Or does he tell the sailors to throw him into the water because he knows their fear of committing such a deed (cf. 1:13-14)?

One thing is certain: Jonah comprehends the LORD's ways. In fact, as soon as the prophet is thrown into the sea, the tempest calms down (1:15).

Jonah is not like the pagans. He does not panic like they do. He does not think that the punishment of a man is the only way to appease God. His prayer is not as ineffective as

---

[18] In addition to the adjective "great", the Hebrew text uses the verb "fear" twice as an emphasis.

theirs, because when he finally prays, at the bottom of the sea, the LORD immediately responds to his request (2:3). Jonah is a prophet. His knowledge of God is excellent, and he knows that God's anger is directed at him. Of course, the entire crew is threatened by the storm, but the sailors are not as innocent as one might think. Didn't they welcome the prophet despite knowing that he was fleeing from the LORD (*"For the men knew that he was fleeing from the presence of the LORD, because he had told them")* 1:10).[19] Thus, he who shelters a sinner also takes his sin upon himself. Many accounts confirm this principle.[20] The solution proposed to the sailors is quite simple. They must separate themselves from the sinner they have sheltered and do it as quickly as possible, so they must throw him into the sea. Jonah is the LORD's prophet and announces the truth.

It is also possible that Jonah is continuing his wrestling match with the LORD. God wants to punish his prophet because the latter does not want to go to Nineveh to give the Assyrians one last opportunity to repent and be saved. Thus, by his sacrifice Jonah shows God that he is ready to give his life to save the pagans. Jonah is not xenophobic; he does not hate all foreigners. He is even ready to sacrifice his own life to save a certain number of them. What Jonah cannot accept is that God pardons sinners who are *as bloodthirsty* as the Ninevites. Jonah is not against mercy and pardon. He objects to the *unlimited* extent of God's love.

Does Jonah think that he could give God a bad conscience with his sacrifice? Does he tell him: "You want to kill me because I am not prepared to save pagans, but you are prepared to kill a crew who is less guilty than the Ninivites?" Is this emotional blackmail? This is not impossible. Jonah is digging his heels in with his objection to the LORD, and wants to teach him a lesson. Imagine a child who is so angry at his father that he asks evil men to throw him overboard

---

19 It is not certain if Jonah already confessed this prior to embarking, but several indications suggest he did: cf. footnote 8 p. 91.

20 For example, in Judges 20, Benjamin is decimated for having supported Gibeah, and Israel loses its first two battles for having placed its confidence in the Levite (D. Arnold, *Le livre des Juges*, p. 341-342).

before the father's eyes. Wouldn't this exert terrible pressure on the father to intervene and save his son?

We note that Jonah does not throw himself overboard. He does not want to commit suicide. He does not want to disobey an order from the LORD. He simply wishes to express his feeling of injustice to God.[21]

The Pagans' Reaction: 1:13-16

> *13 However, the men rowed desperately to return to land but they could not, for the sea was becoming even stormier against them. 14 Then they called on the LORD and said, "We earnestly pray, O LORD, do not let us perish on account of this man's life and do not put innocent blood on us; for You, O LORD, have done as You have pleased." 15 So they picked up Jonah, threw him into the sea, and the sea stopped its raging. 16 Then the men feared the LORD greatly, and they offered a sacrifice to the LORD and made vows.*

The sailors do not follow Jonah's advice immediately. They seek a solution other than the prophet's death. Do they admire the straightforwardness of Jonah, who hides nothing from them, even at the risk of his own life? Are these men good by nature? Even though Jonah's behaviour puts them in danger, the sailors pardon his error and make an effort to save him.[22] Are the sailors sceptical of the solution Jonah proposes? Perhaps they do not think that Jonah deserves death because they ask God afterwards not to hold them responsible for an *innocent's* death (1:14).

---

21 One could blame Jonah for being inconsistent, because he first refuses the call to this mission, then refuses to transgress the divine order on respecting life. Nevertheless, the two divine orders are not of the same type. The first consists of trying to save a third party, the second consists of taking someone's life. Thus, to refuse to heal someone is not equivalent to killing him, even if both gestures lead to the same end. The driver of a car who refuses to stop to provide first aid to someone who has had an accident is not guilty of the same crime as someone who runs over a pedestrian.

22 Hauser p. 27.

The sailors are probably afraid to lay hands on a messenger of the Creator God. Even if the storm unleashes itself against him, this does not mean that God wishes him to perish. Perhaps they must simply row him ashore to allow him to continue his mission. The storm's increasing fury proves the contrary.

It is possible that the notion of a fugitive slave played a role in the sailors' reflection.[23] Jonah presents himself as a *servant* of the LORD who is fleeing far from his master. In a way, he is a sort of fugitive slave. Among the pagans, the law demanded that a fugitive slave be returned to his master. He who did not do so was considered a thief and those who harboured escaped slaves were subject to severe punishment. International laws extended these measures across national borders. By receiving Jonah, the sailors are in the wrong towards the LORD. They must therefore return the prophet to his master. That is what they do by attempting to return him to dry land. Why should they let him perish on the open sea? A dead slave is worth nothing. The storm's increasing intensity indicates to them that the master of the heavens and the oceans is not satisfied with their course of action. He wants his servant immediately, and because both the land and the sea belong to him, the sailors must throw Jonah *into the sea*. Perhaps they also think that Jonah's master is so angry that he wants to punish his servant with death.

"...and the sea stopped its raging." As soon as the deed has been carried out, the divine anger subsides. God is satisfied by the gesture. The sailors express their fear of the LORD.[24] The men see only God's judgment, i.e. that he who disobeys the LORD must die. Jonah's salvation immediately afterwards is hidden from their sight, because the fish swallows him not on the surface but unseen, in the depths of the sea (see also p. 70).

---

23 Robert J. Ratner "Jonah, the Runaway Servant" p. 281-305.

24 This is the second time the narrator underscores the sailors' fear (1:10, 16), but the first time that he links it directly to the LORD ("they feared the LORD greatly"). The sailors' terror is mentioned at the centre and at the edge of a section which concerns the sailors (see p. 40).

The book of Jonah underscores the extent of God's mercy towards men, but it also teaches that this mercy is never automatic. God is remorseful–that is, he is prepared to pardon sinners–insofar as they are repentant. Because the sailors have turned away from sin by turning away from the sinner, they are saved. In contrast, Jonah, who remains rebellious, is cast into the foaming waves of God's wrath.[25]

[25] This principle holds true for all men, even for prophets, as the book of Kings teaches (1 Kings 13:1-32; 20:35-36).

CHAPTER 2

JONAH'S REPENTANCE

The LORD's Intervention: 1:17

> *And the LORD appointed a great fish to swallow Jonah, and Jonah was in the stomach of the fish three days and three nights.*

Is this verse part of Chapter 1 or Chapter 2? English translations[1] attach it to Chapter 1; thus, Chapter 2 begins with Jonah's prayer. On the other hand, French[2] and German[3] Bibles divide Chapter 2 at this verse, clearly indicating that the fish's intervention is a sign of grace (which is the theme of Chapter 2) and not judgment (which was the theme of Chapter 1). Jonah is not swallowed by a sea monster to be chewed and eaten, but to be saved. "The fish serves more as a cradle than a tomb."[4]

---

1 KJ, NIV, NEB, NASV, Living Bible, Good News, Amplified Bible.

2 Seg, Dar, Col, Sem, TOB, Jér, FC.

3 Luther, Zwingli, Schlachter, Elbenfelder, Menge, Hoffnung für alle, Bibel in heutigem Deutsch.

4 "This is not the dragon holding Andromeda captive whom Perseus must fight… nor the 'angry whale' of Jacques Prévert. Nor is it—despite the identical terms used—the 'great fish' emerging from the waters of the Tigris, in the story of Tobit, who threatens 'to swallow' the lad (Tb 6:2). The animal sent by YHWH does not devour the prophet, but instead saves him from the waves by gathering him and holding him in his protective interior, as if in a cradle rather than a tomb; he transports him–at no cost, whereas Jonah had had to pay for the voyage by ship–and finally puts him ashore. This tame animal, this instrument of providence, is really harmless; it obeys to the letter, as did the she-ass of Balaam or Elijah's crows. A difference must be made between the swallower and the devourer; the latter dismembers, the former does no harm." (Couffignal: "Le Psaume de Jonah" *Biblica* 71 [1990] p. 543).

The reference to *"three days and three nights"* immediately signals that a period of grace has been granted to the prophet. The miracle is enormous, but the account remains quite succinct. It states neither the name of the fish, nor the manner in which Jonah remains alive, nor how he was able to determine the length of his underwater stay. The narrator concentrates on spiritual questions rather than material ones. He underscores that the LORD is the origin of the miracle. It is he who commands the fish to intervene, just as in the past when he ordered the wind to blow (1:4). The narrator is then interested in Jonah's prayer (2:1-9); the words express the prophet's spiritual state and his relationship to the LORD.

Material matters are secondary, but they are not negligible. God works with his Creation: Jonah is used to save the Ninevites and an animal is used to save Jonah. The wind was also used to recover the prophet. The speed with which the wind and the fish obey the LORD is offset by Jonah's tenacious refusal. Humanity's basic problem is moral and not physical.

Much ink has been poured on the subject of the type of fish it might have been. The question has been dealt with in the introduction (p. 85-87), which helps us stick to the thread of narration, because this question does not influence the account's comprehension. We simply note that it is not surprising that the narrator does not mention the name of the fish. Who could have done so? The sailors probably did not see it swallow Jonah, because he was already foundering in the depths. The prophet could only see the fish from the inside, and in the dark!

The calculation of the days is rarely dealt with by the commentators. How could Jonah know the exact duration of his stay inside the fish? He had neither a watch nor any contact with the exterior. The period is precisely reported and is therefore important, because it echoes the three days' march through Nineveh (3:3) as well as the "three days and three nights" which Jesus spent in the tomb (Mt 12:40)[5]. A number of replies are imaginable. For example, if Jonah had been cast up on the banks of the Promised Land, he would have easily been able to determine the length of his absence, because Jewish life was punctuated by the weekly Sabbath.

The prophet's survival in the fish is a problem which is partly linked to the type of fish which swallowed Jonah. Some commentators suggest that Jonah was unconscious during most of his sojourn there.[6] However, the text emphasises the opposite with Jonah's overflowing activity, which starkly contrasts his previously passive state.

The First Words of Jonah's Prayer: 2:1-2

> *1 From inside the fish Jonah prayed to the LORD his God,*
> *2 and he said,*
> *"I called out of my distress to the LORD,*
> *And He answered me*
> *I cried for help from the depth of Sheol;*
> *You heard my voice".*

Chapter 2 marks a radical change in the prophet's attitude towards the LORD. Whilst the first chapter is characterised by contention and muteness, the second is characterised by appreciation and abundant, if not to say excessive, verbal

---

5 Jesus did not remain in the tomb for 72 hours, because he died at the end of the afternoon and rose again in the morning before dawn. There are at least 40 hours between Friday evening and Sunday morning. Even if the crucifixion is placed at Thursday afternoon (the reference to a great Sabbath in John 19:31 could express two successive days of holiday), twelve hours are still missing. The Jews had the habit of counting part of a day as a whole day. The expression "three days and three nights" is probably "an idiomatic Hebrew expression which covers either the whole or part of three days and three nights. This expression could thus mean one entire day plus the end of the previous day and the start of the next one." (Kuen p. 135-136).

6 "If we admit that Jonah spoke his prayer of recognition towards the end of the three days, we can suppose that he was unconscious during most of the preceding time; perhaps he was already in that condition when he was swallowed by the great fish." (*NCB* p. 783)

communication. The reader goes from a verbal desert to a flood of words. The prophet's monologue is so intense that words follow each other and repeat themselves without leaving any room for anyone else. If God remains silent, it is not because he is absent or irritated, but because Jonah does not leave him time to intervene. The prophet's need to express his joy is too important. The man who has remained silent in his rebellion must now speak, as if to make amends for his long silence. The prophet's words also let him reveal his feelings, because until now, the narrator has not described a single one, giving the impression that the man was made of steel.

The first words addressed to the LORD *precede* the intervention of the fish (2:2). Jonah cries out to the LORD when he is surrounded by the waters and is about to drown. Jonah is on the brink of death when he turns to the LORD, who hears him and delivers him. The narrator holds back an important piece of information here as well as elsewhere (1:10; 4:2). This method accentuates the suspense and pushes the reader to reflect. He is compelled to re-read the text, which is enriching (see Literary Characteristics).

The LORD works toward the salvation of mankind. He desires to reach the greatest possible number of people, even men as perverted as the Ninevites; he is prepared to save his prophet from drowning. Yet salvation, albeit very generous, is never unconditional. Men must repent to be saved. The condition is the same, both for great sinners (the Ninevites) as well as men of God (Jonah). A period of grace is granted to each. The time can be a bit longer or shorter, announced more or less clearly, but man must repent within this space of time. Jonah does it at the last possible moment, when he is at death's door. This suffices, because a fish is ready to intervene and swallow Jonah should he repent.

One should not conclude from this that man can calmly live in sin, knowing that he can repent at any time and shall receive God's pardon. The length of the period of grace is rarely known and stubbornness in sin often hardens souls to the point that they lose their receptiveness to God at the instant of death. How many men have neglected God and foundered in their indifference? This is never the case with Jonah. From the very start to the end of the account, Jonah cares about the LORD. His revolt is never based on indifference or carelessness (even when he sleeps in the ship). His contention stems from his zeal for justice. The prophet contests the breadth of God's love.

Jonah's sin seems insignificant when compared to the sins of men who are as bloodthirsty as the Ninevites, but his transgression is not negligible. A sin is a sin, and all sins must be punished. Thus, God is prepared to kill his prophet because of his disobedience. This may seem excessive, but that's the way it is. The wages of sin is death (Ro 6:23), and the only road to salvation must pass through repentance. On the other hand, the gravity of any transgression against an order of the LORD means that sin can only be expiated by death. That is why Christ had to die to save mankind. There was no other option. That is also what the apostle Paul declares in the letter he writes to the church of Rome:

> *For all have sinned and fall short of the glory of God, being justified as a gift by His grace through the redemption which is in Christ Jesus; whom God displayed publicly as a propitiation in His blood through faith This was to demonstrate His righteousness, because in the forbearance of God He passed over the sins previously committed; for the demonstration, I say, of His righteousness at the present time, so that He would be just and the justifier of the one who has faith in Jesus. (Romans 3:23-26).*

One might ask why Jonah needed to be punished so swiftly–a few days after his revolt–whilst the Ninevites had escaped God's wrath after decades, even centuries, of iniquity. On the one hand, divine judgment begins with the house of the LORD, because we always ask more of him who receives more. On the other hand, Jonah is a prophet and the LORD manifests himself through such men. Jonah must announce divine justice, even if it is at his own expense.

Jonah's prayer marks a complete turnabout in the prophet's attitude. Jonah suddenly loosens his grip during an arm-wrestling match.[7] This change of behaviour by the prophet is so radical and the change of style between Chapter 1 and 2 so intense–we go from prose to poetry, and from the third person to the first–that a number of commentators consider this psalm as a later addition. Besides, they say, how could Jonah have been able to express his gratitude when he was not saved but rather imprisoned in the belly of a sea monster?[8] But Jonah is a man of faith who knows the LORD.

---

7 Some commentators think that Jonah already prayed on the ship, when he was dozing, or when the captain gave him the order to do so. But this would contradict the story's progression. Jonah's prayer is a complete reversal of his previous attitude.

8 For Spangenberg (p. 507), there are many dissonances in the psalm. Jonah says that God hurled him into the deep (2:3), but the reader knows from the account that the sailors did it upon his request. Jonah says he is banished from the LORD's sight (2:4), whereas he is the one who fled. He expresses his desire to see the temple again, but this contradicts his attempts to flee far from the LORD's sight. Jonah criticises those who reject the true God for idols (2:8), but the idolatrous sailors reject their idols and pray to the true God (1:14), whilst he behaves like a pagan. Some authors speak of Jonah's hypocrisy. But could he be such a rogue under these circumstances and hope to fool God? Jonah is "the son of truth", and he is anything but a hypocrite.

Smelik (*The Literary Function of Poetical Passages in Biblical Narrative. The Case of Jonah 2:3-10* p. 149) on the other hand feels that the purpose of the psalm is to rectify a false impression which the narrative text of Chapter 1 may have left. "Poetical passages such as Jonah's psalm give the author the opportunity to rectify a possible but incorrect interpretation of the text on the part of the reader." (p.149). According to Smelik, Jonah cannot be unfaithful to the LORD. "By inserting the psalm, the author rebuts the view that Jonah is a disobedient servant of the Lord, even an unbeliever: a prophet who sings this text from the belly of a fish cannot be unfaithful to the Lord. There must be another explanation for his recalcitrant behaviour." (p.149). Jonah did not go to Nineveh so as not to betray his nation.

It has been suggested that the prophet's sudden joy negates the account's historicity: "From the simply literary point of view, the hymn about the actions of grace, which is not appropriate to the situation, suggests the hypothesis of an artificial composition of the book. This objection is difficult to resolve for someone who is allegedly preserving the objective facts; such jubilation coming from a man who has been buried alive is incomprehensible." (Feuillet col. 1113). But Kenneth M.

The prophet discerns the LORD's act of salvation behind the fish's intervention. Thus, God will bring to an end that which he has begun, because God is tenacious, even obstinate, particularly regarding his plans of redemption.

> *28 And we know that God causes all things to work together for good to those who love God, to those who are called according to His purpose. 29 For those whom He foreknew, He also predestined to become conformed to the image of His Son, so that He would be the firstborn among many brethren; 30 and these whom He predestined, He also called; and these whom He called, He also justified; and these whom He justified, He also glorified. (Romans 8:28-30).*

The change of style in the psalm does not manifest a foreign body within the account, but a radical change in the prophet's attitude. Jonah is no longer contesting and demanding, but shows gratitude and submission.[9]

The psalm is composed of two parts. The first is a long eulogy by the prophet (2:2-7); the second consists of a brief commitment (2:8-9).

Jonah's Eulogy: 2:2-7

> *2 "I called out of my distress to the LORD,*
> *And He answered me*
> *I cried for help from the depth of Sheol;*
> *You heard my voice.*
> *3For You had cast me into the deep,*
> *Into the heart of the seas,*
> *And the current engulfed me*
> *All Your breakers and billows passed over me."*

Craig replies: "So much attention is paid to the differentiation between poetic prayer (2:2-9) and the prose frame…that it is not surprising that some similarities and points of convergence were neglected." (Jonah and the Reading Process, p. 111).

9 We note that Jonah is probably praying as he lies inside the fish—he who, while lying in the ship, had received the order to rise and pray. (1:6).

4 So I said, 'I have been expelled from Your sight
Nevertheless I will look again toward Your holy temple.'
5 "Water encompassed me to the point of death
The great deep engulfed me,
Weeds were wrapped around my head.
6 I descended to the roots of the mountains
The earth with its bars was around me forever,
But You have brought up my life from the pit, O LORD my God.
7 While I was fainting away,
I remembered the LORD,
And my prayer came to You,
Into Your holy temple."

The rescue from drowning is described in detail, because it constitutes four-fifths of the psalm. The prophet expresses himself freely, holding nothing back, and repeats his words at will, using synonymic terms and expressions. In a few rare cases, he uses the same words; thus the expression *"your holy temple"* appears twice (2:4, 7).[10]

The poetic genre lends itself to emphasis, because Hebrew poetry is based on the repetition of ideas. Poetry is also a literary tool used to express emotions, petitions, requests, pleas, the cry of the heart. Jonah speaks of *distress* similar to a voyage to *the realm of the dead* (depths of the grave) (the two lines of verse 2 are synonyms); he confesses that he *was fainting away* inside (v. 7). The verbs *call* and *cry* (v. 2) testify to the acoustic intensity, even if Jonah, avoided opening his mouth to cry out because he was in the water! Whatever the case, his voice *was heard by* the LORD (v. 2). Other terms or expressions also evoke the death that Jonah skirted: deep (*mesôla* v. 3), to the point of death (v. 5), great deep (*tehôm* v. 5), pit (v. 6). There are also *"roots of the mountains"* and *"the earth with its bars"* which definitely imprison Jonah (v. 6). His spiritual distress is evoked by the fear of having been rejected by the LORD: *"you had cast me into the deep"* (v. 3), *"I said, 'I have been expelled from your*

[10] The other repeated words are: the LORD (3 times: 2:2, 6, 7), soul/life (*nephesh*: twice: 2:5, 7), engulf/bar in (*cabab*: twice: 2:3, 5).

sight" (v. 4). Despite all of these gloomy terms, the psalm is not a funeral oration, but a hymn of praise. Jonah brushes death, but escapes, and his gratitude equals the danger he has experienced. His joy focuses on the fact that his communion with the LORD has been re-established and that he will still be able to worship his God in the *"holy temple"* (v. 4). His commitment, which ends the psalm, also reflects his gratitude (v. 9).

Some readers might think that the ideas expressed here are presented without any precise order. Yet a structure results from Jonah's words. His praise is formed in two parts made up of 30 Hebrew words each, punctuated by the expression *"your holy temple"* (v. 4, 7). Each of these parts is subdivided into two sections which evoke the newfound communion between Jonah and the LORD (v. 4 and v. 7) as well as the deliverance from physical danger (v. 3-4 and v. 5-6). The order of these two domains is reversed between the two parts, which gives the ensemble the form of a chiasmus.

A.1	Jonah cries out to the LORD who hears him	v. 2
B.1	Jonah is saved from drowning	v. 3-4
B.2	Jonah is saved from drowning	v. 5-6
A.2	Jonah cries out to the LORD who remembers him	v. 7

According to certain commentators, this psalm is only an amalgamation of bits and pieces borrowed from different psalms, the product of a later compiler who produced this patchwork for insertion into this work. For example, Couffignal quotes 15 verses drawn from 12 different psalms, but his analysis is far from convincing, because none of the verses is taken up in its entirety.[11] Jonah was most probably

[11] "This 'psalm' is made up of several verses drawn from the canonical Psalter; one recognises formulas which have become clichés: 'I called to the LORD, ...he answered me... he listened to my cry... what I have vowed I will make good... I will look again toward your holy Temple..." (Couffignal p. 545). Despite this mixture of transposed bits and pieces, this author feels that "the compiler has succeeded in creating a work which stands the test." The suggested "parallels" make

so imbued with Biblical thought, particularly the psalms of David, that he spontaneously prayed in these Biblical "categories" during his ordeal.[12] Have we not already shown how well Jonah knew the LORD? Those who memorise Scripture accumulate a precious hoard for times of trouble.

"You had cast me into the deep" (v. 3). Jonah does not blame the LORD for having punished his rebellion, because he knows that every sinner must be judged. With his words the prophet simply recognises that his troubles have been commanded by the LORD. His words show no bitterness. He makes no demands. He simply expresses his thanks for having been pardoned and for being able to continue to live in God's presence: *"yet I will look again toward your holy temple"* (v. 4).

The mention of the temple is a bit surrealistic for some commentators. Isn't Jonah trying to flee the face of the LORD? Why does he now think of the temple whilst he is inside the fish? This reference is important because it is repeated literally twice (v. 4, 7). Note that both times, Jonah points out that it is the "holy" temple, i.e. the building set apart by the God of the covenant to represent him. The holy temple contains the ark of the covenant by which God is committed to pardon the repentant sinner who turns to him (cf. 1 Kings 8:44, 48). Thus, despite the sin, complete communion with the LORD can be regained.

Jonah's Commitment: 2:8-9

> *8 Those who regard vain idols forsake their faithfulness, 9 But I will sacrifice to You with the voice*

---

it possible to draw up the following list: verse 3 (Ps 18:7; 120:1), verse 4 (Ps 24:2; 42:8), verse 5 (Ps 31:23), verse 6 (Ps 18:5; 69:3), verse 7 (Ps 30:4), verse 8 (Ps 5:8; 42:6; 88:3; 107:5), verse 9 (Ps 31:7), verse 10 (Ps 3:9; 42:5). Seven psalms are attributed to David, two to the son of Korah and two are anonymous. H.L. Ellison (p. 364), who dates the psalm at the 8th century, mentions 20 quotations derived from 16 different psalms. Between the two authors, only 7 quotations are identical, which underscores the arbitrary method of procedure.

12 "This chapter is filled with allusions to other psalms; this shows to which degree Jonah knew Scripture." (Feinberg p. 139).

> *of thanksgiving that which I have vowed I will pay, salvation is from the LORD.*

In the belly of the fish, after having expressed his gratitude for being saved, Jonah promises to carry out his vows. The narrator does not specify the nature of his commitment, but the context immediately makes us think of the prophet's calling to go to Nineveh. Jonah's prompt obedience to the second missionary call confirms his good disposition (3:1-3).

We would like to emphasize that Jonah makes his plans *in the belly of the fish*, when he has not yet been freed. Is this the reflection of great faith? Despite the extended stay in the monster, Jonah knows that God will free him in due course, because the LORD has caused the fish to intervene specially to save him. The "three days and three nights" would thus only be necessary to give the fish time to carry the prophet to the shore. But this extension of the stay can also be understood differently. Could it be a way of testing the prophet's faith? Or a way of putting pressure on him, because the LORD does not wish to release his prophet as long as the latter has not accepted his mission? The wrestling match between the LORD and Jonah thus continues. After three days, Jonah gives way and makes his commitment. God releases him immediately, because he trusts the prophet's words. The "son of truth" is recalcitrant, but he is not a liar. He will carry out his vows.

The reference to idolatry may be surprising (cf. v. 8). Why mention it? Is it to provide a context for his vow? Because the pagans reject the true God, they cannot be saved. Jonah is going to announce judgment to the Ninevites. Does the reply lie in Jonah's reticence towards his mission? By keeping him captive, God is forcing his hand. Jonah capitulates, but not before having expressed his opinion: the idol-worshipers cannot be saved. Jonah will thus go to Nineveh, because its idolatrous inhabitants cannot avoid the announced judgment. Does Jonah expect God to take his thoughts or his request into account? This seems possible if we look at his disappointment after pardon has been granted to the Ninevites

(3:10). However, by saving the Ninevites, God does not oppose Jonah's thoughts. The inhabitants of the Assyrian megalopolis are saved *because* they have turned to God. Thus, the practicing idol-worshipers–i.e. those who trust in their idols–cannot be saved. Jonah is right in saying *"Salvation is from the LORD"* (v. 9).

Jonah's last words are fundamental. They summarise the book's entire teaching. By saying them, Jonah perceives only one aspect of that truth. The prophet thinks that the idol-worshipers should have died because they neglected the LORD's grace, but basically, the declaration goes much deeper. Not only does the LORD pardon the repentant sinner, but over and above the repentance, he establishes conditions favourable to salvation. He sends messengers to exhort the sinners to convert. The New Testament further reinforces this thought: Christ takes condemnation upon himself, and the Holy Spirit works in the heart of the chosen to make them sensitive to the words of the Gospel. Salvation in all its fullness is the work of God. *"Salvation comes from the LORD."*

Epilogue of the Fish: 2:10

> *10 Then the LORD commanded the fish, and it vomited Jonah up onto dry land.*

Jonah is freed as soon as he has pronounced his commitment. Here as well as elsewhere in Scripture, God gives an old "quarreler" the means to accomplish his mission. Jonah is freed from his "guardian" (and rescuer) who vomits him onto dry land. A few centuries earlier, Gideon, who had asked for only one sign to be sure that the LORD was truly calling him (Jug 6:17), had seen the angel of the LORD disappear in a flame. As for Moses, he had first experienced miraculous signs which he was able to produce to convince the people, and then received the help of his brother Aaron to communicate them better (Ex 3-4). This principle often holds true even today. God's powerful hand acts in such a way that the faithful respond to his call.

The account of Jonah's "liberation" is succinct. There is no need to explain the event in detail, because the fish responds instantly to the Creator's order.[13] It shows no hesitation, contrary to Jonah.

Some commentators[14] advance different hypotheses regarding the prophet's physical appearance. The gastric acid in the fish's stomach would have caused the prophet's skin to become wrinkled and swollen, and would have discoloured or blanched it. These signs, confirmed by the miracle of the fish announced to the Ninevites, would explain why everyone paid Jonah such heed. There is no indication in the text to confirm such a suggestion. Neither the prophet's appearance nor the account of the miracle–which no-one knew about, except Jonah–but solely the preaching of God's judgment upon the bloodthirsty city is the origin of the Ninevites' repentance.

The commentators also debate about the landing place. There again, the text remains silent. A place near the port where Jonah embarked would be logical.[15] The sailors would doubtless have tried to turn back, because they felt that the fugitive should be returned to his master, the God *of Israel*. However, their main worry was simply to anchor somewhere. Furthermore, the storm had probably disoriented them, and we know neither the time span between their departure and the start of the storm nor the duration of the hurricane. In addition, Jonah spent three days in the fish. There are too many variables to propose any kind of hypothesis. Lastly, one could suppose that the LORD, who had insisted so much on the success of Jonah's mission, had ordered the fish to spew him out at a favourable location, be it near the road to Nineveh, be it close to the port of departure to prevent the

---

13 According to Sherwood (Cross-Currents in the Book of Jonah, p. 51) who quotes Holbert, the fish was sick of housing a hypocritical prophet. However, the vomiting is not the result of a moral evaluation by the fish (!), which would be lamentable because Jonah is an upright man, but rather of God's command.

14 Zlotowitz p. 117.

15 Schrader p. 647, Gaebelein p. 96.

prophet from losing too much time trying to orientate himself. The ease with which Jonah gets to Nineveh (a voyage described in one verse: 3:3) shows that the issue of the landing point is negligible compared to Jonah's sin. Once again, problems on the material level are insignificant compared to spiritual and moral ones.

CHAPTER 3

JONAH'S COMMITMENT

The LORD's Second Call: 3:1-2

> *1 Now the word of the LORD came to Jonah a second time, saying: 2"Arise, go to Nineveh the great city and proclaim to it the proclamation which I am going to tell you."*

The LORD's second call is almost identical to the first (cf. 1:1-2). The first is made up of 20 Hebrew words, the second of 21. Thirteen of these words are common to both. The differences are minor and concern two points. To begin with, the expression *"a second time"* replaces the information on Jonah's origin (*"the son of Amittai"* 1:1). Although they are different, these two expressions play a similar role. They bring the reader back to familiar information. In the first case, the name of Jonah's father had permitted the reader to identify Jonah with the prophet contemporary to Jeroboam II (cf. 2 Kings 14:25). In the second, the expression *"a second time"* leads the reader to the beginning of the book and to the first two chapters.

The second difference between the two calls deals with the manner in which Jonah's mission is formulated: instead of crying against Niniveh because *"its wickedness has come up before me"* (1:2), Jonah must proclaim *"the message I give you"* (3:2). To all appearances, the message is identical, but the attentive reader remarks that the negative connotation of the first call is absent from Chapter 3. The Ninevites' evildoing is no longer mentioned and Jonah no longer needs to preach *against* Nineveh. In Chapter 3, Jonah must preach *to* the Ninevites (the preposition is different, e.g. the narrator uses *al* instead of *el*) and simply announce God's message. This last remark is even more pertinent when we realise that

God's grace manifests itself progressively within the account (see p. 31-33).

The similarities between 1:1-2 and 3:1-2 make it possible to *set the boundaries* of the book's two larger sections. These two sections have several resemblances (which appear to be announced by the analogy of God's order). Thus, we can state that at the start of these sections, the prophet speaks to the pagans and not to the LORD (Chapters 1 and 3), then, secondly, he speaks only to the LORD (Chapters 2 and 4). At the same time, the antithetical parallels are even more pronounced than the similarities. Chapters 1-2 take place to the west of Israel, at sea, whereas Chapters 3-4 take place in the Promised Land, on pagan ground.[1] The first section mentions the prophet's contention (Chapter 1), then his repentance and communion with the LORD (Chapter 2). The second mentions similar elements, but in reverse order: first the prophet's obedience (Chapter 3), then his disagreement (Chapter 4). (See the Chapter on the book's structure, p. 39-51.)

Jonah's Obedience: 3:3-4

> *3 So Jonah arose and went to Nineveh according to the word of the LORD. Now Nineveh was an exceedingly great city, a three days' walk. 4 Then Jonah began to go through the city one day's walk; and he cried out: "Yet forty days and Nineveh will be overthrown!"*

Jonah rises *and obeys*. It is a complete contrast to his reply to the first call (1:3). Whilst his efforts to get to Tarshish are described at length (Chapter 1) and the voyage was nevertheless aborted, the journey to Nineveh is summarised in one verse. As soon as Jonah's departure is mentioned (*"Jonah arose"*), the narrator moves to the description of Nineveh's grandeur (*"an exceedingly great city, a three days' walk."*). In the blink of an eye, we move from the first act of

1 More precisely, to go west, Jonah would first have to travel to Jaffa, *south* of Galilee; to travel east, the prophet would have to go *north* before entering Mesopotamia, because the caravan routes followed the Fertile Crescent.

obedience (the prophet gets going) to the gaze of a voyager who discovers his destination from afar. When there is obedience, difficulties appear derisory, to the point that the author considers them not worth mentioning. Yet a voyage to foreign lands lasting several weeks was not a trifling matter (cf. Ez 8:21-23, 31).[2]

In Chapter 1, the author had said that *"Jonah rose up to flee to Tarshish from the presence of the LORD"* Now he says: *"Jonah arose and went to Nineveh according to the word of the LORD."* (3:3). The expressions *"rose up to flee... from the LORD"* and *"went ...according to the word of the LORD"* are antithetical: complete disobedience on the one hand, absolute obedience on the other.

The three days' march describing Nineveh (3:3) echoes the "three days and three nights" spent in the belly of the fish (1:17). The similarity is even greater when we know that the name "Nineveh" means "the house of the fishes."[3] Jonah goes from one house of fish to the next. The only difference is that the stay in the latter seems to have been shortened due to the Ninevites' ultrarapid repentance (see below, p. 137), and that the stay in the fish may have been prolonged due to the prophet's reluctance to accept his mission (see p. 121, 129). We also note that the two stays in a "house of a fish" were—humanly speaking—very risky. The people who emerge from a sea monster alive are the subjects of a miracle, and who would dare enter a city of criminals to condemn their behaviour? Jonah emerges unscathed from both places.

The "three days' walk" poses a problem for some commentators who feel that Nineveh's size is exaggerated. But before speaking of a historical error, we must be certain

---

2 According to Schrader (p. 647), the voyage to Nineveh would have taken one month by camel caravan or on a donkey and perhaps five weeks on foot.

3 "The cuneiform sign for Nineveh combines that of the fish and that of a dwelling (house). Therefore 'dwelling-fish' would be a haggada for Nineveh." (North p. 128). According to Assyriologist Donald J. Wiseman ("Jonah's Nineveh" in *Tyndale Bulletin* 30 [1979], "The logographic rendering of the name, used as an emblem of the goddess Nina, or Nanse, is *ès* + ku_6 (nûnu) i.e. house of fishes or masses."

of the expression's meaning. The term has a variety of interpretations.

Some consider the distance a person can walk in a period of three days, but are we looking at the city's diameter or its perimeter[4]? Although Nineveh's fortifications had a perimeter of 12 kilometres, Jonah did not restrict his message to the wealthy who lived within the city walls, but communicated it to everyone.[5]

It is also possible that the three days refer to the day of arrival, the day to attend to business and then the day of departure. This would mean three days of procedure, i.e. three steps which every stranger on a diplomatic mission must follow. Thus, Jonah is the ambassador of the LORD encharged with a precise message, but it is difficult to see how this statement of "three days" could be connected to the city's size.

Some commentators make reference to the "Assyrian triangle", a region defined by three cities which lay between 15 and 40 km apart (Korsabad, Nineveh, Nimrod). The term "Nineveh" would therefore not apply to one single city, but to an entire district. Nowadays, don't we also speak of the City and "greater London", the city and the state of New York?[6]

---

4 Zlotowitz p. 120. The archaeologist Wiseman (p. 37) states that he knows of "no description of an ancient city's size using the mass of its walls."

5 According to Archer (*A Survey of Old Testament Introduction* p. 302, footnote 8): "It is inconceivable that an ancient author, no matter who he was, could have supposed that any city in the world was so vast that it would take three days to go from one end to the other." A vigorous man can cover 85 to 100 km in three days, the distance from Jerusalem to the Sea of Galilee. No compact city ever had such dimensions; if that had been the case, it would have harboured up to 30 million inhabitants."

6 "It is true that André Parrot has suggested that Jonah's description could have meant the triangle of cities which lie in a compact group from Korsabad to the north, to Nimrod in the south, which is around forty kilometres. In this case, the number of 120,000 inhabitants would not be an exaggerated estimate of the population." (Lacocque p. 42 cf. Parrot, *Nineveh et l'Ancien Testament*, p. 63-64; Jonah 4 :11). According to Wiseman (p. 39), "The area which stretched 30-60 miles in diameter could be included in the Hebrew text, whose use of *ninua*

The three days' walk could represent the number of days required to preach the message at all the public places of the city, e.g. the days needed to accomplish the task.[7] Tourist guides also indicate the number of days it takes to visit the main monuments.[8] When the Persian king Artaxerxes asks Nehemiah how long his voyage will be (Ne 2:6), he inquires about the period of absence he will need to accomplish his task and not how long the journey will take.[9]

We also note that the *"three days' walk"* (v. 3) stand parallel to Jonah's *"one day's walk"* (v. 4). The prophet never had to walk through the entire city, because the city repents as soon as the message is announced.

Jonah announces that the city shall be *overthrown*. The verb *hâpak* (turn, turn around, change, destroy) could evoke Sodom and Gomorrah's destruction, where the same verb is used three times (Ge 19:21, 25, 29). But the expression *"Yet forty days and Nineveh will be overthrown."* is ambivalent. It announces either the city's destruction or its repentance. In fact, the *"forty days"* can be understood as an ultimatum[10]

---

in each case could not, like an Assyrian text, distinguish between the metropolis proper (*alninua*) and the whole district (*ninuaki*) or both (*alninuaki*), since prefix and postfix determinatives are not normally employed in Hebrew as in Assyr." Alexander (*Tyndale OT Commentaries* p. 57-58) points out that the expression "the great city" also appears in Genesis 10:11-12 to describe Nineveh and the entire region composed of four cities. Keil (*The Pentateuch*, quoted by Alexander) concludes: "It follows that the four places formed a large composite city, a large range of towns, to which the name of the (well-known) great city of Nineveh was applied, in distinction from Nineveh in the more restricted sense."

7 "Preaching at street corners requires long stops at each point where the message is proclaimed." (Archer, *A Survey of Old Testament Introduction*, p. 298).

8 "In our opinion, 'city of three days' should be taken in the sense of a Michelin Guide: you need three days to rapidly take in and view all of the monumental marvels with which the city is bulging." (North p. 140).

9 Schrader p. 648.

10 Feinberg p. 144 ("Forty is the number employed in Scripture in relation to testing"); Schrader p. 648. One could quote the flood (Ge 7:17), Moses on Sinai (Ex 24:18), Elijah at Horeb (1 K 19:8), Jesus during the

and the verb *hâpak* could refer to a change of heart, a profound repentance by the Ninevites.[11]

Is Jonah conscious of the double message he announces or does he proclaim salvation to the Ninevites unknowingly? Obviously, the first proposition applies to Jonah, because the prophet is not blind but stubborn. He understands the LORD's ways better than anyone else, but he has difficulty accepting them completely. Jonah is not a Caiaphas who unwittingly prophesies (cf. Jn 11:49-51). He is the son of Amittai who has the courage and integrity to announce the whole truth. If Nineveh does not repent, it shall be destroyed; if it repents, it shall be saved. A deadline of forty days is granted to the city for a reform.

Jonah's message consists of only five Hebrew words—it is hard to be more succinct. Does the narrator reflect the prophet's displeasure to carry out his ministry? (Jonah carries out his task, but nothing more. The message is complete: judgment and grace, but it is reduced to its simplest expression.) On the contrary, does the narrator wish to underscore the speed of the Ninevites' repentance? Five words are enough to change their lives. The two possibilities are consistent with the nature of the account.

The message's ambiguity (judgment or grace) is in tune with a book written to make people think. The author also wishes to unveil divine grace progressively. He moves from

---

temptation (Mt 4:2). The Greek Septuagint translation speaks of "three days" and not of "forty days."

11 This verb is sometimes used this way (Halpern p. 87); for example, to express Saul's change of heart at the start of his ministry (1 Sa 10:6 9): *"God gave him* (hâpak) *another heart"* (KJ), *"God changed his heart"* (NASV, NIV). Jé 13:23 speaks of a leopard which cannot change its skin (i.e. its identity). "The use of the verb *hâpak* to evoke the destruction of Nineveh allows a play on words on an important theme of Chapter 3: it can be understood that the city will be 'overturned' (destruction), if the inhabitants do not 'turn about' (conversion) to God." (Legrand p. 20). "As Rashi notes, God strategically uses a word about turning around that can itself be turned around and can speak simultaneously of forgiveness and disaster. And the word of overturning just keeps on turning." (Sherwood "Cross-Currents in the Book of Jonah" p. 70).

the announcement of judgment only (1:2) to the exclusive announcement of grace (4:11).

The People's and the King's Humbling: 3:5-6

> *5 The Ninevites believed God. They declared a fast, and all of them, from the greatest to the least, put on sackcloth. 6 When the news reached the king of Nineveh, he rose from his throne, took off his royal robes, covered himself with sackcloth and sat down in the dust.*

The Ninevites' repentance is immediate and complete. Right after the announcement of the message, the entire population, through all social levels (*"from the greatest to the least"*), humbles itself. The people do not wait until the king is informed of the warning, and they take all the necessary measures. The state of emergency is felt by all, before it is even officially proclaimed. Nevertheless, such an important message would certainly have been rapidly communicated to the monarch.

The king takes the message just as seriously as his subjects. As soon as it is announced, he repents and clothes himself in mourning before ordering all of his people to do the same. The king steps off of his throne, which is the place of honour and glory, (*"rose from his throne"*) to go and sit *"down in the dust"*, a place of humiliation and lamentation. He exchanges his royal robes, another sign of honour and glory, for sackcloth, the symbol of misery.[12]

Some commentators feel that the repentance was not deep, or they even deny that it ever took place[13], whereas others try

---

[12] The elements are presented in chiasmatic form (inversion of the facts): noble place and clothing, then poor clothing and habitation. They also follow a chronological order, as the king must rise before removing his cloak, then must put on his new clothing before sitting down again.

[13] Some sceptics point out that the Ninivites' "repentance" is not mentioned in any profane writing and that it left no trace in Assyrian history. In view of such objections, one must recall that historical data for this period are often very biased. Onc can at least note an interest in monotheism under Adad-Nirâri III (see footnote 16 below). According to Feinberg (p. 146), there is no doubt that the repentance was sincere,

to explain it with a set of particularly favourable circumstances. Major difficulties could have rendered the Ninevites more receptive to Jonah's preaching. A period of political instability due to military defeats, certain climatological phenomena–famine, earthquake[14], solar eclipse[15]–is mentioned. The trouble with these hypotheses is that Jonah's voyage to Nineveh cannot be dated with any certainty and that precise knowledge about the situation in Assyria during the end of the 9th and 8th centuries B.C. is rare.[16]

They also point out that the Assyrians had the habit of welcoming foreign preachers.[17] They were considered as itinerant ambassadors (there were no permanent diplomats) and their services were often called upon in times of great cataclysms, just as local and foreign specialists are consulted today to help resolve extreme situations.[18] Some

---

otherwise God would not have accepted it. It was perhaps of a limited duration, as is the case with most repentances of nations.

14 The prophet Amos, who also carried out his ministry during the reign of Jeroboam II, mentions a great earthquake (Am 1:1).

15 The Assyrians regularly dated special events according to solar and lunar eclipses. This practice allows modern historians to establish dependable dates for the chronology of the Near East with different cross-checks.

16 See "The Historical Context of the 8th Century" p. 80. Archer (*A Survey of Old Testament Introduction*, p. 299-300) proposes two periods to explain the Ninivites' conversion. First, the period of Adad-Nirâri III (810-783): "It is well known that this king restricted his worship to the god Nebo, and that he thus was closer to 'monolatry' than any other Assyrian sovereign." After that, the reign of Assurdân III: "If Jonah had come to Nineveh twenty years later, under the reign of Assurdân III (771-754), he would have found a population psychologically ready for a complete catastrophe; in fact, a severe plague had ravaged the city in 765 and a total eclipse of the sun had occurred on June 15, 763. Another scourge had followed in 750." Wiseman defends the same position (p. 50-51). See also point 3 p. 125.

17 Donald J. Wiseman: "Jonah's Nineveh" in *Tyndale Bulletin* 30 (1979) p.43 "Men from one city-state entering another for specialist advice whether political, medical or for religious purposes are now attested from the Mari texts onwards." p. 47.

18 "Cuneiform literature is extremely rich with requests for pardon and psalms of penitence: calamities, illnesses and omens of similar

commentators even suggest that the account of the sojourn inside the fish had already reached Nineveh before the prophet. With such a reputation, the prophet would naturally have been listened to, even more so seeing that the name of Nineveh refers to fish ("the house of fish") and that local tradition (set down in writing around the year 280 by Berosius) confirms that the Assyrian arts and sciences were brought to the Persian Gulf by a deity who was half-fish, half-human, named Oannes in Greek.[19]

All of these explanations attempt to make the Ninevites' repentance more plausible, but the legitimacy of such a procedure is questionable. On one hand, the explanations rest on very fragile foundations. (We have already pointed out that the fact that the sailors probably did not even see Jonah being swallowed by a fish.) On the other hand—and this is a major objection—these explanations contradict the text. The author never makes an effort to justify the Ninevites' repentance. On the contrary, this repentance is presented as

---

misfortunes led Assyrians and Babylonians to turn to the Deity in an attempt to appease it by means of prayers and rites of expiation: they would have easily believed any diviner's portents, and, according to Schaumberger, it becomes totally comprehensible that Jonah's prediction of Nineveh's ruin would have made a deep impression on its inhabitants." (Feuillet col. 1111).

19 According to Eugene H. Merrill ("The sign of Jonah" in *JETS*, 1980, p. 23-30, primarily p. 27 and 29), "It is unlikely that the story of his marvellous transportation and deliverance failed to become known and even to precede him. In any event, the confinement in the stomach of the fish with its attendant and obvious deleterious effects would surely mark Jonah physically and could not fail to make him the object of utmost curiosity. And of course one cannot rule out the possibility of divinely appointed witnesses who not only saw the regurgitation but bore testimony to it in Nineveh and all along the way." Preiswerk (p. 10-11) and Schrader (p. 667) share the same opinion. But James Swetnam replies ("Some Signs of Jonah" in Biblica 68 [1987]): "On the contrary, there is no indication in the Book of Jonah that Jonah's being in the belly of the sea monster was known to the Ninevites at the time of his preaching. Such knowledge would undermine the strictures of Jesus against his adversaries for their refusal to believe: he could hardly compare them unfavourably to the Ninevites if the Ninevites had a motive for belief which Jesus' adversaries lacked."

being something exceptional. The reader is surprised by its speed and wide acceptance.

A number of commentators see it as a derision of the Hebrew people who have remained unmoved by their prophets' appeals, contrary to the Ninevites who immediately welcome Jonah's words. We are not satisfied with this ironical reading of the account. In fact, does any nation exist who would have reacted as favourably to the word of the LORD as the Ninevites? Their attitude is not only superior than the Hebrews', but also unique; it is the best possible one. Never in the history of mankind had a people responded so rapidly, so extensively and so favourably to the preaching of God's word, condensed into five words and transmitted by a reluctant messenger. The exegete should not weaken what the author has made obvious, even if it raises questions. The reader should let himself be challenged by the Bible message. The disgrace of the cross should never be attenuated, but proclaimed. The Ninevites' repentance is exceptional, so it must be announced and meditated upon! Couldn't it be a foreshadowing of the exceptional extension of God's grace to the pagans when the Holy Spirit would come over them (cf. Acts 2)? Would God have sent his prophet by the name of "dove" (Jonah), because he had decided not only to offer an opportunity of salvation to the Ninevites, but also to provide them with the means of salvation? The divine renewal in the Ninevites' hearts is not explicitly mentioned in Jonah, but it is at least suggested. At any rate, it would perfectly explain the mass repentance of the Ninevite sinners (cf. Ez 17:1-24; Rom 11:25-27, 32).

The reference to the "king of Nineveh" (3:6) also poses a problem, because profane writings speak of the king of *Assyria*, and not the king of *Nineveh*. Several explanations have been proposed:

1. It could be that the author wished to keep the framework of his account as simple as possible. Rather than adding an additional proper name which had no further bearing on the account, he identifies the

sovereign as the king "of Nineveh" rather than the king of "Assyria".[20]

2. Certain cities were the "private" property of kings. Ahab is called the king of Israel (1 Kings 20:43), but also king of Samaria (1 Kings 21:1); Ben-Hadad, king of Syria, is also called king of Damascus (2 Chr. 24:23). The city of Nineveh could have therefore depended directly on the king of Assyria.
3. He could also be the city's governor, because the king's residence was not at Nineveh at the time of Assurdân (771-754), but rather at Asshur or Calah. Nineveh did not become the capital of the empire until the reign of Sennacherib (705-669).[21] And there was a period during which the king of Assyria and his empire were weak (783-745). According to Paul Ferguson[22], the governors had great power and only granted the king nominal approval. The term "king" (*melek*) was used for local governors. All of the steles of this period which have been found were erected by governors (which shows their importance). "This period of scarcity in royal record was called the 'forty lean years' by W.W. Hallo." (Ferguson p. 311).

The King's Decree: 3:7-9

7 Then he issued a proclamation in Nineveh: "By the decree of the king and his nobles: Do not let any man or beast, herd or flock, taste anything; do not let them eat or drink. 8 But let man and beast be covered with sackcloth. Let everyone call urgently on God. Let them

---

20 "No ancient author who mentions Nineveh in the accounts in our possession (in Acadian, Hebrew, Greek or Latin) appears to have ignored the fact that the city was the capital of the Assyrian empire. It would be naive to suppose that an author living in 430 B.C. would not have known that the king of Nineveh was also the king of Assyria." (Archer, *A Survey of Old Testament Introduction*, p. 298).

21 Schrader p. 648.

22 "Who was the 'King of Nineveh' in Jonah 3:6?" in *Tyndale Bulletin* 47.2 (1996) p. 301-314.

give up their evil ways and their violence. 9 Who knows? God may yet relent and with compassion turn from his fierce anger so that we will not perish?"

The king issues a decree to impose repentance upon his entire kingdom. He does know that the people have spontaneously humbled themselves and that both nobility and commoners have clothed themselves with signs of repentance (3:5). The decree might seem superfluous to some, but the king wants to make sure that none of his subjects will escape this humbling. Is he aware of the fact that one member's sin can corrupt the entire body? This bloodthirsty monarch who had hardened his conscience in the past has suddenly become hypersensitive to evil. The imminent threat and danger of divine judgment make him react with the energy of despair. Be it of their own will or by force, the nobles add their signature to the king's to show the unanimity of power.[23]

The king wants to do everything humanly possible to make God change his mind and his decision. He is not satisfied with imposing a fast on all men, rich and poor, but also includes the animals. The narrator makes a list of the royal decisions. The words are repeated, and increasingly intensify the depth of repentance.[24] Three words are used for the animals to express the entire scope: beasts, herd and flock. The first term is general and covers the quadrupeds, because birds, fish, insects and reptiles would not have been included in the fast. The two other terms, herd and flocks,

---

[23] If the king had only limited power (see point 3, p. 125), the reference to the governors could be easily understood. "The king of Assyria may have been the king of Assyria only in name. His effective control over large parts of his kingdom may have been surrendered to powerful provincial governors; he may have been effective king of Nineveh, but of little more: hence his title in the book of Jonah... The decree is issued as the decree of the king and his nobles. In his decree he has to acknowledge the power and influence of known nobles." (Paul J. N. Lawrence: "Assyrian Nobles and Jonah" in *Tyndale Bulletin* 37 [1986], p. 131). See also Alexander, *Tyndale OT Commentaries*, p. 79.

[24] "The exaggeration is at its peak here and manifests the radical change of the Ninivites' behaviour: it reinforces the contrast between Jonah's reluctant behaviour (ch. 1) and the obedient attitude of Nineveh's inhabitants and leaders" (Legrand p. 21).

state precisely that domestic animals are implied, whatever their size.[25]

It is a total fast, with absolutely no food or drink. On the subject of food, different verbs are used for the animals (eat) and for men (taste). The latter must abstain from all nourishment, because the first meaning of the verb for taste (*tiâ'am)* is "to try, or to evaluate, with the tongue, normally with consultation if the flavor is suitable" *TWOT* no. 815).

The strongest impressions must be communicated visually and audibly. All creatures are covered in sacks and must cry to God at the top of their lungs. No excuses are made to mitigate the sin. On the contrary, the decree emphasises the degree of the evil committed. It mentions the evil ways and the acts of violence attached to guilty hands. Everyone is ordered to make a radical change.

No pressure is exerted on God, no demands are made, because the only thing the guilty deserve is judgment. But although pardon can never be required, it can, on the contrary, be requested, and that is what the king of Nineveh does.

The king has no assurance whatsoever of pardon. He expresses his uncertainty with a question: *"Who knows?"* Did he perceive only judgment in Jonah's words? Does he doubt that criminals can be pardoned? He certainly does not know the extent of God's mercy the way Jonah does (4:2). The king can therefore only throw himself into the hands of the Creator God in the hope that he will also be a merciful God. He does this in the same way as the sailors, who had also implored God to spare them from his wrath (1:6, 14).[26] This is the same attitude that any unbeliever should have when he realises his sinful state. This is the only way that pleases God, because he alone can save, he alone can pardon sin.

---

25 According to Herodot, the Persians had the custom of including animals in their mourning rites (Nouvelle Bible Segond, study edition, footnote p. 1155).

26 "The phrase 'Who knows?' should be read as an echo to the 'perhaps' pronounced by the ship's captain in Jonah 1:6. It is actually the hope of possible salvation which concludes the king of Nineveh's speech." (Legrand p. 21).

The LORD's Change of Heart: 3:10

> *10 When God saw what they did and how they turned from their evil ways, he had compassion and did not bring upon them the destruction he had threatened.*

The Ninevites' repentance leads to the suspension of God's judgment. The expression *"he had compassion and did not bring upon them the destruction he had threatened"* is a problem for several commentators. How can God repent? Is he flexible, capricious, unstable, and indecisive? Is he bad and does he harbour evil thoughts which force him to make amends? God's repentance also raises questions about the credibility of his word. Are God's prophecies–be they promises or judgments–trustworthy?

Few commentators dare suggest that God was morally indebted, because this would directly contradict the many Scripture affirmations of God's holiness, perfection and unchanging nature. Some commentators seek a solution in the prophet's imperfections. Origen felt he could resolve this difficulty by stating that Jonah did not transmit God's message, but rather his own. Instead of simply announcing that *"its wickedness has come up before me"* (1:1), he could have announced Nineveh's destruction on his own initiative (3:4). In fact, the narrator never puts words of destruction *("Forty more days and Nineveh will be overturned!")* in the LORD's mouth.[27] Such an approach unnecessarily defames Jonah. The son of Amittai does not mislead anyone, he is honest and truthful. His word can be trusted, now and in the future. Had not the storm calmed down according to the prophet's announcement (1:12, 15)?

---

[27] "Origen first proposes a simple solution: Jonah announced Nineveh's destruction by its own leader. He deduces in Jonah 3:4 (LXX) that Jonah only had to repeat what God had commanded him the first time: 'That the Ninivites' evildoing had risen up to him'. Thus, the 'condemnation which had not been carried out appeared to be Jonah's doing rather than God's' " (Johannes Roldanus: "Usages variés de Jonah par les premiers Pères" in *Figures de l'Ancien Testament chez les Pères* [Cahiers de Biblia Patristica 2], 1989, p. 171-172).

We must seek the solution to "God's remorse" elsewhere. A difference must be made between the goal and the means. God's plans are unchangeable. God seeks not the sinner's death, but his salvation. Thus, the announcement of judgment is preferable to a judgment without prior warning, because the former gives the sinner one last opportunity to repent. God does not change his basic plans for man: the plan consists of judging the sinner and pardoning the repentant sinner. If the guilty party repents, God will withdraw his judgment. If man does not do so, judgment will be carried out according to what has been announced. The driver of an automobile who wants to drive through a place will follow the road, but may occasionally modify his trajectory by moving right or left to avoid an obstacle. Nevertheless, his basic route remains unchanged from start to finish. In the same way, God's action depends simultaneously on his principles and men's reactions.

Salvation and pardon are thus possible no matter what the extent of the sin and no matter who the individual is. The Ninevites were great sinners and were a bloodthirsty people. They were pagans and there were many of them, hence they were far from the LORD and without any consideration for him. Yet these people repented. That is enough for God to grant them pardon, because the LORD is *"a gracious and compassionate God, slow to anger and abundant in lovingkindness, and one who relents from sending calamity"*, as Jonah states in Chapter 4 (v. 2).

God's pardon is thus linked to men's repentance, but the repentance must be serious. God knows men's hearts, so he cannot be fooled. He knows the difference between true and false repentance. The Ninevites had pleaded guilty all the way down the line. They had committed to lead fully reformed lives and not just to express some regrets. God therefore pardons their great sins. The Ninevites' earnestness is exemplary. Although they risk ridicule, they do everything to witness their humility.

Their attitude clashes with that of other men who, despite being reinstated by God, only repented in part. King Saul sometimes regretted his behaviour (1 Sa 15:24), but he never changed his life, because he was more preoccupied with his contemporaries' opinion than with God's will (1 Sa 15:30).

Following these remarks, it is obvious that we do not share the opinion of the commentators who downplay the depth of the Ninevites' repentance. Even Jesus mentions the reality of this repentance (Mt 12:41; Lk 11:32).

CHAPTER 4

JONAH'S OBJECTIONS PUT INTO WORDS

Jonah Displeased by His Mission's Success: 4:1-2

> *1 But it greatly displeased Jonah and he became angry. 2 He prayed to the LORD and said, "Please LORD, was not this what I said while I was still in my own country? Therefore in order to forestall this I fled to Tarshish, for I knew that You are a gracious and compassionate God, slow to anger and abundant in lovingkindness, and one who relents concerning calamity."*

Jonah's account could have ended at Chapter 3, because the prophet's mission had been achieved and God had reached his goal. Yet the book of Jonah is not only interested in the Ninevites' repentance, but also in the ties which unite the prophet to the LORD.[1] This relationship is agitated, rough, stormy, even turbulent. Until now, the narrator has not expressed any negative feelings about the prophet and has been content with describing his rebellious behaviour (cf. Chapter 1). In the last chapter, the narrator penetrates to the very heart of the conflict-ridden relationship. He twice

---

1 "If man, unaided by the Spirit of God, were writing this account, it would probably have concluded with the close of Chapter 3." (Feinberg p. 148). "In some respects the fourth chapter is the richest portion of the book of Jonah." (Gaebelein p. 113). The fourth chapter shows that the book is not primarily a missionary treatise, but a didactic work.

reports Jonah's desire to die (4:3, 8)[2] and four times (4:1, 4, 9) he uses the verb irritate (*charah*) ("This word is related to a rare Aramaic root meaning 'to cause fire to burn,' and to an Arabic root meaning 'burning sensation,' in the throat." TWOT no. 736). He begins the chapter with three words which mark Jonah's profound dissatisfaction. Literally, "this unfolded *(yara')* a great *(gadôl)* displeasure *(ra')*" (4:1).[3]

Why is Jonah so angry about his mission's success? Hasn't he just helped accomplish the greatest religious awakening in the history of mankind? Which contemporary preacher wouldn't be in seventh heaven if he were to have even one-tenth of Jonah's success? The astonishment which the prophet's reaction provokes is particularly evident when a reader discovers the account for the first time. The prophet's reticence to carry out his mission could be explained by the dangers linked to a perilous mission. Jonah escapes the Ninivite cauldron unscathed. The criminals to whom he speaks do not kill him or attack him. It is even likely that they thanked him for his message.

The reason for Jonah's anger (and why he flees his first calling) is expressed in verse 2. Jonah did not want the Ninevites to escape divine judgment. This verse is without a

---

2 In Chapter 1, Jonah's proposition to be thrown into the sea can be *interpreted* as a suicide attempt, but it remains an interpretation (which is debatable: see p. 100). In Chapter 4, Jonah puts his intention of dying into words.

3 The verb *yara'* expresses deep sorrow/pain, which makes someone tremble or shiver, and fills them with dread. It expresses Abraham's feelings when Sara asks him to chase away his son Ishmael (Ge 21:11-12); Hannah's grief when she is faced with her barenness and the mockery of her rival Peninna (1 Sa 1:8); Samuel's anger when the people reject him and demand a king (1 Sa 8:6); Saul's jealousy when the women admire David ten times more than he (1 Sa 18:8); God's wrath after David's sin with Bathsheba (2 Sa 11:27). The word *ra'* is translated in a very different fashion, but always in a pejorative sense: harm, misfortune, displeasure, deformity, disaster, pain, ugliness, wickedness, criminal, ferocity. The adjective great *(gadôl)* is used fourteen times in Jonah and further increases the intensity of the sentiment expressed. We also note that this chapter is the only one which expresses Jonah's joy, a *great* joy (4:6), which appears at the centre of the chapter (see structure p. 41).

doubt the most important one in the book, because it explains the core idea of the account and summarizes the book's theological teaching in just a few words. The veil around Jonah is lifted, but only partially, because certain questions remain. Why didn't Jonah want the Ninevites to be saved?[4]

1. Did he hate foreigners to the point of wanting to see them all perish? But his gesture of salvation towards the sailors excludes any notion of general xenophobia (1:12).
2. Did he hate the Assyrians because of the evil they had wrought on Israel in the past? Yet the Assyrians had not oppressed Israel in recent decades except on a few rare occasions.[5]
3. Did he opportunistically prefer to see a potential enemy of Israel disappear from the map?
4. Did he resist the idea that God extended his compassion to people other than Israel because of egoism and chauvinism?
5. Was he afraid that the Ninevites' repentance would make Israel's hardening even more evident? In fact, the Israelites had been warned by several prophets in the past, but the people remained insensitive to any appeals for repentance. Would the Ninevites' sincerity hasten Israel's judgment? This is Jewish tradition's point of view.[6]
6. Did his sense of justice prevent him from accepting a manifestation as great as God's love? This answer seems to fit best with his special mission (see p. 106), but the many different explanations related to Jonah's irritation are developed in our commentary on verse 3,

---

4 Person (p. 171-186) provides a list of ninety entries to show how commentators have understood verse 2.

5 An eight-year oppression by Cushan-rishathaim is mentioned at the start of the period of Judges (Jug 3:8-10). During Ahab's reign (874-853), a coalition of twelve kings had repulsed the Assyrian troops in 853 at Qarqar on the Oronte river, more than 200 km north of Damascus, but this battle is not mentioned in Scripture.

6 See footnote 10 p. 92.

> because this verse underscores the prophet's suicidal depression and not only his irritation.

When Jonah mentions his flight to Tarshish, he uses two words to describe it: *qadam* and *barah*. The second poses no problem, because it is translated with "flee" in all versions. On the other hand, the word *qadam* ist interpreted differently. Some versions read it as a chronological reference ("I *first* wanted to flee..." Dar, Jér, KJ), others as a reference to Jonah's "discernment" ("that is what I wanted to *prevent*..." Seg, Col, NEG, Sem, Schlachter); some as an indication of speed ("I *hurried* [or *hastened*] to flee..." BCF, TOB, Parole vivante, ASV). The verb appears 26 times in the Old Testament. It means: encounter, come face to face, confront, pass in front of.[7] The phrase could also be translated thus: "that is why I *confronted* (you) by fleeing to Tarshish" or "that is why I wanted to *contest* you by fleeing to Tarshish."

The second part of verse 2 mentions divine mercy. It is the book's core statement. The sentence consists of fourteen Hebrew words (two times seven, the number of perfection). It contains a five-word introduction which testifies to the fact that Jonah knew God from the very start: "because I-knew that you-are a-God."[8] Five statements about God follow: the first two are formulated in one word ("compassionate and-merciful"), the two which follow consist of two words ("slow to-anger", "and-abundant in-lovingkindness") and the last of three words ("and-one who-relents-in calamity"). These five statements underscore the LORD's goodness toward the repentant sinner. The thought is repeated (which is a sign of emphasis in Hebrew thinking); it is also increasingly developed (from one word to three), which is another way of underlining a topic's importance.[9]

---

[7] "The root *qdm* incorporates two basic concepts: first, (and most often) 'to confront (meet) someone with either a good or bad intent,' and second, 'to precede someone or something either temporally or geographically.'" *TWOT* no. 1988).

[8] When a Hebrew word is translated with several English words in our text, the words are connected with hyphens.

[9] This credo on divine goodness is mentioned seven times in Scripture: "The LORD, the LORD God, compassionate and gracious, slow to

Jonah Pouts: 4:3-5

> *3 "Therefore now, O LORD, please take my life from me, for death is better to me than life." 4 The LORD said, "Do you have good reason to be angry?" 5 Then Jonah went out from the city and sat east of it. There he made a shelter for himself and sat under it in the shade until he could see what would happen in the city.*

"*...please take my life from me...*" What a strange request to address to the God of life! Is Jonah so dissatisfied with the turn of events that death is "*better to me than life*"? But why is Jonah so discouraged?

1. Is he distraught for Israel's sake? Because the Ninevites' repentance makes the Israelites' hardening of heart more obvious, seeing as they have remained unaffected by many prophetic exhortations, the divine judgment upon the chosen nation shall be all the more severe. But Jonah knows the LORD. He knows that he will judge each one according to his own sin and not by someone else's behaviour. Another people's repentance or hardening will not change Israel's sin in any way.
2. Is he disheartened to see a people as cruel as the Ninevites remain on the international scene and continue to remain a military threat to Israel? Yet Jonah knows that the chosen people's weakness is never linked to the enemy's power, but instead to its own sin. Furthermore, due to the Ninevites' ethical conversion, any military campaign of theirs is temporarily set aside.
3. Does he fear being considered as a traitor after returning to his country? Salvation borne to a nation which is an enemy of Israel might not be viewed kindly by certain Hebrew nationalists. But Jonah's

---

anger, and abounding in lovingkindness and truth;" (Ex 34:6-7; Ne 9:17; Ps 86:15; 103:8; 145:8; Joel 2:13; Jon 4:2). The reference to pardon is not always present; it is sometimes expressed differently.

voyage to Nineveh has shown that he does not fear men's anger.

4. Is he confused about the fact that his prophesy has not come about? Does he already have doubts that his prophetic ministry in Israel might be compromised?[10] However, a true prophet does not worry about the opinion of men. In addition, his prophecy included the possibility of repentance.
5. Does he regard the Ninevites' repentance as a personal failure? Despite all of his efforts, Jonah was not able to prevent God from accomplishing his project. Jonah is dejected and loses all joy of life.[11] Yet he is not a man who is easily discouraged.
6. Is he so jealous about God's love manifested to another people (cf. Ro 11:11, 14) that he resorts to emotional blackmail? Jonah asks God to let him perish to make him intervene in his favour. Children sometimes accuse their parents of not loving them, with the sole aim of forcing them to express their love.[12]
7. One explanation similar to the previous one, but which we find better (and which is the one which we uphold), returns to the analysis of the prophet's contention following the first calling. Jonah had already fled to show his disagreement with God's project. Now, after a successful mission, Jonah takes up this contestation again, but expresses it verbally this time. The form changes, but the essence remains the same. This time around, Jonah does not turn his back and remain silent, but instead addresses God directly. He asks him to take his life. Such proposals addressed to a loving God are intended to inflict pain.

---

[10] Frolov (p. 90-91) thinks that Jonah sees his career ruined, because people will consider him to be a false prophet.

[11] Guillaume (p. 21) suggests that Jonah reproaches God "for having him take such a long voyage for nothing (if he had gone to Tarshish, the result would have been the same)".

[12] Several commentators compare Jonah to the elder son in the prodigal son parable (Lk 15:25-32: Gaebelin p. 116).

> Jonah thus wishes to hurt God, because he has been hurt himself. The wrestling match with God continues, but shifts from the strategic level to a more emotional one. Jonah knows that the LORD's soft spot is his compassion. By asking the LORD for death, he pokes his finger in the wound. He expresses to God his feeling of not being loved by him. In summary, he tells him: "By forcing me to carry out a mission which is unpleasant to me, you worried about the Ninevites more than about me. Certainly, you have saved the Ninevites, but you have lost me."

"The LORD said, 'Do you have good reason to be angry?'" God responds to the verbal aggression with a question. Jonah is far too upset with the LORD to hear anything else, and would turn a deaf ear to any discussion. A question, on the other hand, makes people reflect. Three Hebrew words suffice to express it. This question is an invitation to a dialogue, because God would have plenty with which to seal the lips of his prophet, who borders on impertinence. The LORD grants space for the dialogue, because he not only desires to save the Ninevites, but also wishes to instruct his prophet in order to win him over to his cause.

What can Jonah answer? Is it appropriate to be irritated with the LORD? Obviously, a negative reply to the latter question is expected. The question even seems superfluous, yet it not only has the advantage of making Jonah reflect, but also the readers who might be engaged in a foolish disputation with the LORD.

For the moment, Jonah refuses to answer, as he is leaving the city to install himself to the east. No matter, the LORD is patient. Is he not *"slow to anger and abundant in lovingkindness"*? He will wait for the favourable moment to pursue the discussion he has started with his prophet.

Why does Jonah set himself up to the east of the city? Normally, the prophet would have returned home because his mission had been completed. The construction of a lean-to testifies to an intention to stay in the country for some time, but no-one would imagine that the prophet wished to live amongst the repentant Ninevites forever. Jonah thus leaves the city and installs himself at his (provisional) abode outside of Nineveh. He wishes to remain in the area as an observer, to "*see what would happen in the city*".[13]

Jonah is obstinate. He does not give an inch in his wrestling match with the LORD. To return home would mean to accept defeat—namely, admitting that God was right in sparing the Ninevites. Jonah wants to stay on location to see how the situation develops. Does he doubt the sincerity of the Ninevites' repentance? Whatever the case, their enthusiasm for their newfound morality will soon lose steam. Jonah tells himself that all he needs to do is to catch the first signs of unfaithfulness so he can ask the LORD to carry out the judgment he had announced. It doesn't matter if his vigil is short[14] or long; Jonah is prepared to wait as long as is necessary. The construction of a shack is evidence of his wish to prolong his stay. Jonah installs himself to *the east* of the city, i.e. in the direction opposite to the way back, to indicate to the LORD that he absolutely does not intend to return home.[15]

The LORD Prepares an Object Lesson: 4:6-8

> *6 So the LORD God appointed a plant and it grew up over Jonah to be a shade over his head to deliver him from his discomfort. And Jonah was extremely happy about the plant. 7 But God appointed a worm when dawn came the next day and it attacked the plant and it withered. 8 When the sun came up God appointed a*

---

[13] Certain commentators think that Jonah is doubtful and has difficulty believing in divine pardon. The prophet was "waiting desperately for the end of the 'forty days'" (*NCB* p. 785) to see Niniveh's destruction. But Jonah was a man of faith who perfectly understood the extent of divine pardon (cf. 4:2).

[14] Some rabbis say that Jonah wanted to wait for 40 days to see if the people returned to their sinful ways.

[15] Note that Nineveh is located in the Mesopotamian plain, at the foot of the high Persian plateau which rises to the east of the city. The area east of the city provided an elevated position which was an ideal observation post.

> *scorching east wind, and the sun beat down on Jonah's head so that he became faint and begged with all his soul to die, saying, "Death is better to me than life."*

Because Jonah refuses to speak (whilst at the same time communicating his disapproval by his behaviour), God meets up with his prophet by using non-verbal language also. God's action is divided into two steps.

To begin with, God does something good for Jonah, because the vine[16] provides more shade than the lean-to[17]. The prophet reacts immediately. For the first time in the account, Jonah is happy. He even feels *great* joy. The adjective *gadôl* (great) appears 14 times and multiplies by ten the importance of feelings and events. The prophet's reaction is no doubt linked to his interpretation of the miracle. In fact, the plant (or shrub) grows in one night (4:10). Jonah considers this not only as divine intervention, but also as the LORD's approval. Perhaps he thinks that the LORD is encouraging him to remain at his observation post! Perhaps the judgment has only been temporarily postponed and at the slightest sin, pardon will make way for judgment. This interpretation explains why Jonah is joyful for the first time.

---

16 The plant's biological identification is difficult, because the term is a hapax (i.e. a word which appears only once in the Bible). The Darby version simply transliterates the Hebrew term: kikajon. Some versions use the general term "plant" (NASB, TOB, FC), others translate it as "gourd" (KJ) or "vine" (NIV). One must also know that at one time or another, the plant was also identified as a "castor-oil plant", "ivy" (Bernard P. Robinson: "Jonah's Qiqayon Plant" in *ZAW* [1985] p. 390-403). It could be a local climbing plant or a plant with large leaves, because the miracle is not the plant, but rather the speed at which it grows.

17 Several commentators question the plant's usefulness, seeing as Jonah had already built a hut. It is exaggerated to speak of irony here, as some commentators do, because any camper appreciates the shade of a tree in addition to the tent when temperatures are scorching. Jewish tradition proposes the following explanation: "The 'hut' was most likely a provisional shelter made of branches and leaves which would quickly dry and wither in the sun's heat." (p. 136). "Besides, the shade of the kikayon would compensate the uselessness of his hut which provided very little shade." (p. 137).

In fact, in the fish, Jonah was grateful and relieved at being saved, but he still had to carry out a task which was distasteful (to him). Now, he hopes that the LORD is not opposed to rapid judgment of the Ninevites.

The second divine intervention is completely opposite to the first. God destroys the tree which he has miraculously let grow. A harmful worm kills[18] the plant and an easterly wind withers the leaves. The swift destruction of the providential plant, as well as the twofold misfortune (a sort of double witness) is the sign that the mishap has not happened by chance.[19] Furthermore, the hot wind and sun[20] bother Jonah directly.

Jonah is vexed, perhaps less by the heat than by the LORD's actions. He is deeply disheartened, particularly if, on the previous day, he had thought that the LORD approved of an extended stay in Nineveh, and that he was ready to retract his decision to pardon the Ninevites. The prophet asks for death once again. The words are almost identical to those he utters in verse 3, the only difference being that the narrator now presents them in the form of indirect speech rather than a quote. Is it a way to indicate that the gap between Jonah and the LORD has widened?

The LORD's double intervention raises a few questions. Why does God begin by doing Jonah good before doing something bad? Does God play with men? Does he enjoy torturing them? (Best not to accept a gift if one is going to lose it soon afterwards.) Does God go from hot to cold (or from cold to hot in Jonah's case) arbitrarily, simply to lead men astray? Men often wonder about the goodness and justness of divine intervention.

---

18 The verb *nakah* means kill or strike. It is translated as smote (KJ), sting (Jer), chewed (NIV, Seg, Dar, Sem), or attack (NASV, Col, TOB, FC).

19 God is not limited in any way. He sometimes uses large animals and at other times very small ones. His miracles are more or less evident, but the faithful will not doubt the large ones and will not be contemptuous of the small ones. They will be aware of all of the LORD's interventions.

20 Did the wind disperse clouds which temporarily shielded Jonah from the sun?

Some general remarks must be made at this point. God uses the miracle of the vine to instruct Jonah. The author presents the lesson in the last verses of the account (4:10-11). In addition, Jonah's suffering is not deadly, even if Jonah requests death. God neither kills Jonah nor threatens his health. The prophet is just severely inconvenienced, and his discomfort is progressive. Jonah could have been relieved at any point, but to do so he would have had to leave his observation post. The LORD's action is meant to dislodge the prophet from his entrenched position. The LORD is fighting the prophet's stubbornness, not the prophet himself.

We also note that good precedes evil. Does this serve to illustrate that the LORD's goodness precedes judgment? God begins by pardoning the repentant sinner, but if the latter persists in sin, he will end up judging him. The city of Nineveh, spared the first time around during Jonah's time, fell one-and-a-half centuries later, in 612 A.D., before the Medes' and Babylonian armies. The second judgment, which is inescapable, was prophesied by Nahum. Nineveh's history shows that God is not opposed to judgment, but that grace must first be shown, and this grace is plentiful. That is why the time of patience granted to the Ninevites is longer than Jonah's lifespan. The prophet's extended presence at Nineveh is therefore inappropriate.

It is also possible that God provides a lesson connected to the prophet's disagreement. The latter had expressed his faith in God's love (4:2), then disputed this love by asking him to take his life ("you don't really love me, take my life" 4:3). God thus begins by blessing Jonah and letting the vine grow, then retracts his blessing by making the plant wither. Because Jonah is hot and cold, God is the same.[21] The wrestling match continues.[22]

---

[21] Allen mentions that "Jonah's attitude demands of God that he destroy. So God does just that, to see how Jonah likes his theology coming true in the physical realm." p. 233)

[22] A study by Kidner ("The Distribution of Divine Names in Jonah" *TB* 21, 1970, p. 126-128) on the use of God's names in the book of Jonah indicates that the names are distributed throughout the entire length of the account, with "Yahweh" ("LORD") used by Jonah to speak of God

The LORD's Teaching: 4:9-11

> *9 Then God said to Jonah, "Do you have good reason to be angry about the plant?" And he said, "I have good reason to be angry, even to death." 10 Then the LORD said, "You had compassion on the plant for which you did not work and which you did not cause to grow, which came up overnight and perished overnight. 11 Should I not have compassion on Nineveh, the great city in which there are more than 120,000 persons who do not know the difference between their right and left hand, as well as many animals?"*

Because Jonah "deigns" to take up the verbal dialogue again (4:8), God again expresses himself verbally. He almost repeats the question posed at the start of the chapter (4:3), which Jonah never answered (*"Do you have good reason to be angry?"*) but this time, the cause of his irritation is specified: *"about the plant?"*.

Jonah also pursues the dialogue and answers the question this time: *"I have good reason to be angry, even to death."* From his point of view, his irritation is entirely justified. Two elements could explain his reply. First of all, Jonah feels more than ever like the victim of a joke. God offers a gift, then retracts it; he lets his prophet believe that he approves him, then disapproves of him. He has reason to be annoyed. Secondly, the word *charah*, translated as "anger", is etymologically linked to the word for heat (see p. 150). By

---

and "God" used to speak of the relationship the pagans have with the Creator. The only "irregularities" can be found at the end of the book between verses 4:6 and 4:9 (particularly 4:7-9). The word "God" is used to describe the relationship with Jonah. Some commentators see this as a confusion or the fact that there are several authors ("At this point the suspicion may arise that the authorship of Jonah is composite, or its text disturbed. Both views have been taken." p. 127). It could be regarded as a touch of irony by the author, because the passage concerned (4:7-9) reflects only a partial image of God. Thus, the merciless God who dares judge sin is not worthy of being called Yahweh (LORD), the God of the covenant.

drying up the vine, the LORD physically increases Jonah's heat. The prophet thus has a physical reason for being heated.

The wrestling match appears to be more intense than ever. Is the relationship between the prophet and the LORD at an impasse, as the prophet is angered *"even to death"*? Nothing moves on the geographical level: there is no voyage, either to the east nor to the west, nor a three-day march within a city, nor an underwater transport of "three days and three nights". Jonah has constructed his shack and digs in his heels. He has no intention of leaving it, despite the extreme climatic conditions. But Jonah is not only physically frozen; he also appears to be rooted fast mentally, because he is obstinate and wallows in his irritation against the LORD. Once again there is a flagrant contrast between Jonah and the Ninevites. Whilst the former have repented at the speed of light upon hearing five words from the LORD, Jonah continues to exculpate himself.

But hope is not lost, as the signs of a fresh start can be perceived. The LORD gives Jonah a long answer (4:10-11).[23] If the LORD decides to speak in this way, it is certainly because he knows his prophet will listen. The latter has given up his non-receptive attitude.

God teaches Jonah with a parable, which is the method commonly used to reach a hardened heart. Nathan made use of it when he had to rebuke David (2 Sa 12:1-7). Samson sought to teach his contemporaries, who had remained rebellious for forty years, by means of object lessons.[24] Other prophets did the same: Jeremiah, Ezekiel... In the New Testament, Jesus began to speak in parables (Mt 13:3) after scandalous accusations by the Jewish leaders who declared that he drove out demons with the power of the Devil (Mt 12:24). Jesus then accused them of committing an unforgivable sin–the sin against the Holy Spirit (Mt 12:31-32)–and spoke to them about the sign of Jonah (Mt 12:39-41)!

---

[23] This last message of God is longer than the others added together (1:2; 3:2; 4:4, 9), e.g. 39 words out of a total of 73.

[24] D. Arnold: *Ces mystérieux héros de la foi*, p. 232-29; *Le livre des Juges*, p. 239-301.

God's parable consists of a comparison between two situations[25]. On the one hand there is Jonah and the vine, on the other God and the Ninevites. On either side, Jonah or God are troubled by the (actual or planned) disappearance of the vine or the Ninevites. The main difference between the two situations is that the vine didn't cost Jonah anything and that it only "existed" for twenty-four hours. On the other hand, the relationship between the LORD and the Ninevites is presented as one of a father and his children, but also that of the Creator and his creatures, because animals are also involved. The duration and the intensity of the relationship, multiplied by the number of creatures, underscore God's attachment for Nineveh's inhabitants. The prophet could thus identify with God and understand why the LORD was so intent on saving Nineveh[26].

One question which is often debated by commentators concerns the identity of the *"120,000 persons who do not know the difference between their right and left hand, as well as many animals"* (4:11). Are they adults and children, or only children? In the first case, the total population would be 120,000; in the second, Nineveh would have had a population of around 600,000 persons[27]. Because these numbers–particularly the second–seem impossible, some commentators consider them to be fictitious[28].

Three reasons lead us to believe that the reference describes the population in general.

1. The expression is never used to describe children. Wiseman, a specialist of Near East archaeology, categorically confirms this (p. 39): "but there is no

---

25 Raymond F. Person (p. 187-190) quotes nineteen interpretations of the end of the book.

26 According to Allen (p. 234), God essentially said to Jonah: "Your attachment to it could not be very deep, for it was here one day and gone the next. Your concern was dictated by self-interest, not by a genuine love. You never had for it the devotion of the gardener."

27 This position is defended by Feinberg (p. 151) and *BA* (p. 130) among others.

28 Nevertheless, according to some ancient authors (Ctesias, Diodorus and Strabo), Nineveh was larger than Babylon (*BA* p. 123).

evidence known to me of the use of this expression to denote infants."

2. The population size of ancient cities is difficult to assess. There is, however, a precise census which was taken during a great feast at Nimrud (30 km south of Nineveh), which counted 69,574 persons. The surface area of that city was only half that of Nineveh.[29]
3. If God wished to spare the children, why would he have sent Jonah to announce the city's destruction? The mere presence of children in the city would have prevented the judgment (Abraham follows a similar reasoning when he intercedes in Sodom's favour: Ge 18:17-33). In fact, it is the repentance of the guilty which averted Nineveh's judgment (3:10). That is why God was so adamant about instructing the inhabitants of their impending doom. The Ninevites were certainly criminals (1:2), but they completely lacked discernment in the ethical and spiritual realms, just like children who have not yet been instructed[30].

The last verse of the book mentions the greatness of God's love better than all the others[31]. The LORD has compassion

---

29 However, a certain number of outsiders would certainly be included in the population (guest dignitaries and foreign labourers), with the children being excluded. For André Parrot (*Nineveh et l'Ancien Testament*, p. 64), "the indication of *'more than 120,000 persons who do not know the difference between their right and left hand'* does not appear to be exaggerated."

30 Wiseman p. 39: "Many Jewish and Christian interpreters have argued, that this stands for the whole population, who were characterized as unable to distinguish between various forms of religion, especially monotheism (the right) and polytheism seen in nature, and the worship of the constellations which was a mark of the Assyrians. 'The Ninevites deserve compassion as virtual children compared with the Jews'; they were 'spiritual minors'").

31 For Walter B. Crouch ("To Question an End, to End a Question: Opening the Closure of the Book of Jonah" p. 101-112), the main theme of the book is not the Ninivites' repentance. According to Peter Höffken ("Das Ende des Jonabuches" p. 293), the book of Jonah ends with a novel teaching: namely that God gives grace to the Ninivites because of their lack of knowledge and not

with all of his creatures, including animals. This does not mean that God saves all men, but it causes him sorrow to lose some of them (including animals). That is why God seeks to save entire populations in times of special grace. Nineveh is an example of what God carries out on a scale which is significantly greater since the incarnation of Jesus Christ. Jonah's mission is unique in the Old Testament, but it primarily announces the work which God has been carrying out since the coming of the Messiah, because "*...God our Savior... wants all men to be saved and to come to a knowledge of the truth.*" (1 Timothy 2:3-4).

Did Jonah finally accept the full extent of God's love? The narrator says nothing at all about this. However, the absence of an answer does not prevent us from imagining Jonah's reaction. From our point of view, it appears that Jonah ends up fully accepting the LORD's redemptive intention. If not, why would the book have been written? The account depends entirely on Jonah's testimony[32]. In any case, one can rest assured that "the son of truth" took great pains to faithfully report the events which concern himself.

In conclusion, we note that the account ends with a query[33]. God questions Jonah, and in so doing calls upon the

---

because of their repentance. But does the author of Jonah actually contradict himself at the end of the book? Isn't it preferable to think that he is reinforcing his teaching?

[32] Bolin: "This careful attention to the amount of speech in this dispute indicates that for the author there is no clearcut victor in the debate between Jonah and Yahweh over the latter's actions. Each side is given 'equal time', as it were to set forth its position, but in the end the topic remains insoluble... Unlike in Job, there is no indication given in the text that either God or Jonah wins this dispute." (p. 149). Yet Bolin neglects the fact that Jonah begins by speaking a lot, then twice limits himself to a few words only (39 words, 3 words, 5 words), whereas with God, the movement is inverted (3 words, 5 words, 39 words). The length of the last reply gives a clue as to who won the debate.

[33] "The translators almost always refused to translate the verse simply with an affirmation. They put the verb in an interrogative form, or added a question mark at the end of the affirmative sentence. *Segond* and *TOB* dare to place an exclamation point at the end of the affirmation, but they put the verb in the conditional, thus transforming the exclamation into a rhetorical question." (Guillaume p. 23). The

reader at the same time. What would we have answered in the prophet's stead? The LORD's question does not end the dialogue, but instead gets it going again. Do we accept the love which God has shown to the world through Jesus Christ? Have we accepted it for ourselves? Are we ready to share it with others? And in a more general manner, do we welcome God according to the revelation which he has given to mankind, or do we disagree with him on one or several points?

---

book of Nahum, which prophesies Nineveh's destruction, also ends with a question, one which expects a positive reply, just like in Jonah. *"There is no relief for your breakdown, Your wound is incurable. All who hear about you will clap their hands over you, for on whom has not your evil passed continually?"* (Nahum 3:19 NASV).

BIBLIOGRAPHY

------- "Jonas (Livre de)" in *Nouveau Dictionnaire Biblique*, St-Légier, Emmaüs, 1961, p. 408-410.

------- *The Illustrated Bible Dictionary*, Part 2, Leicester, IVP, 1980, p. 806-808.

AALDERS, G. Ch. : *The problem of the book of Jonah,* London, Tyndale, 1948, 30 p.

ADAM, A.K.M. : "The Sign of Jonah : A Fish-Eye View" in *Semeia* 51 (1990) p. 177-191.

ALEXANDER, T. Desmond : "Jonah and Genre" in *Tyndale Bulletin* 36 (1985) p. 35-59.

------- "Jonah : an Introduction and Commentary" in *Obadiah, Jonah, Micah,* Tyndale Old Testament Commentaries 23a, Leicester, IVP, 1988, p. 47-131.

ALLEN, Leslie C. : *The Books of Joel, Obadiah, Jonas and Micah,* in the New International Commentary on the Old Testament, Grand Rapids, Eerdmans, 1976, p. 175-235.

ARCHER, Gleason L. : *A Survey of Old Testament Introduction,* Chicago, Moody, 1964, p. 295-303.

------- *Encyclopedia of Bible Difficulties*, Grand Rapids, Zondervan, 1982, p. 300-302.

ARNOLD, Daniel : *Le livre des Juges : ces mystérieux héros de la foi*, St-Légier, Emmaüs, 2004, 395 p.

------- *Elie entre le jugement et la grâce. Commentaire de 1 Rois 17 à 2 Rois 2*, St-Légier, Emmaüs, 2001, 202 p.

------- *Elisée précurseur de Jésus-Christ. Commentaire de 2 Rois 2-9*, St–Légier, Emmaüs, 2002, 217 p.

------- *Esther : survivre dans un monde hostile*, St-Légier, Emmaüs, 2000, 199 p.

------- *Ruth à la croisée des chemins*, St-Légier, Emmaüs, 2003, 135 p.

------- "Peut-on questionner Dieu ?" in *Promesses* 143 (2003) p. 3-5.

AUNEAU, Joseph : "Un conte théologique et satirique" in *Cahiers Évangile. Supplément* 110 (2000) p. 5-10

AVRIL, Anne-Catherine : "Les données rabbiniques" in *Cahiers Évangile. Supplément* 110 (2000) p. 21-48

BALDWIN, Joyce : "Jonah" in *The Minor Prophets : An Exegetical and Expository Commentary*, vol. 2, ed. Thomas Edward McComiskey, Grand Rapids, Baker, 1993, p. 543-590.

BANKS, William L. : *Jonah the Reluctant Prophet*, Chicago, Moody, 1966, 123 p.

BARILIER, Roger : "Jonas lu pour aujourd'hui" in *Revue Réformée* 126 (1981) p. 49-87.

BARRÉ, Michael L. : "Jonah 2,9 and the Structure of Jonah's Prayer" in *Biblica* 72 (1991) p. 237-248.

BOLIN, Thomas M. : *Freedom Beyond Forgiveness. The Book of Jonah Re-Examined* (Journal for the Study of the Old Testament. Supplement Series 236), Sheffield, Sheffield Academic Press, 1997, 217 p.

BOYER, Frédéric : "Jonas dans la littérature moderne ou l'évangile de la baleine" in *Cahiers Évangile. Supplément* 110 (2000) p. 115-124.

BULLOCK, C. Hassell : *An Introduction to the Old Testament Prophetic Books*, Chicago, Moody, 1986, p. 41-54.

BUXTON, Barclay F. : *The Book of Jonah*, London, Japan Evangelistic Band, s.d., 53 p.

CARROLL, Robert P. : "Jonah as a Book of Ritual Responses" in *'Lasset uns Brücken bauen...'*, ed. K.Schunck, (Beiträge zur Erforschung des Alten Testaments und des Antiken Judentums 42), Frankfurt am Main, Peter Lang, 1998, p. 261-268.

CHRISTENSEN, Duane L. : "Andrzej Panufnik and the Structure of the Book of Jonah : Icons, Music and Literary Art" in *Journal of the Evangelical Theological Society* 28/2 (1985) p. 133-140.

------- "Jonah and the Sabbath Rest in the Pentateuch" in *Biblische Theologie und gesellschaftlicher Wandel. Für Norbert Lohfink*, ed. G.Braulik, Freiburg, Herder, 1993, p. 48-60.

COOPER, Alan : "In Praise of Divine Caprice : The Significance of the Book of Jonah" in *Among the Prophets. Language, Image and Structure in the Prophetic Writings*, ed. Ph.Davis (Journal for the Study of the Old Testament. Supplement Series 144), Sheffield, JSOT Press, 1993, p. 144-163.

COREY, M.A. : *Job, Jonah and the Unconscious. A Psychological Interpretation of Evil and Spiritual Growth in the Old*

Testament, Lanham, University Press of America, 1995, 150 p.

COUFFIGNAL, Robert : "Le Psaume de Jonas (Jonas 2,2-10). Une catabase biblique, sa structure et sa fonction" in *Biblica* 71 (1990) p. 542-552.

CRAIG, Kenneth M., Jr : "Jonah and the Reading Process" in *Journal for the Study of the Old Testament* 47 (1990) p. 103-114.

------- "Jonah in Recent Research" in *Currents in Research : Biblical Studies* 7 (1999) p. 97-118.

CROUCH, Walter B. : "To Question an End, to End a Question : Opening the Closure of the Book of Jonah" in *Journal for the Study of the Old Testament* 62 (1994) p. 101-112.

DAHAN, Gilbert : "L'exégèse médiévale du livre de Jonas" in *Cahiers Évangile. Supplément* 110 (2000) p. 91-100.

DAUBE, David : "Jonah : a reminiscence" in *Journal of Jewish Studies* 35 (1984) p. 36-43.

DEANE, W. J. : *Jonah* (The Pulpit Commentary), London, Funk & Wagnalls, 1906, 102 p.

DÉCLAIS, Jean-Louis : "Jonas en Islam. Une exception chez les prophètes." in *Cahiers Évangile. Supplément* 110 (2000) p. 85-90.

DELL, Katharine J. : "Reinventing the Wheel : The Shaping of the Book of Jonah" in *After the Exile. Essays in Honour of Rex Mason*, ed. J.Barton, Macon, Mercer University Press, 1996, p. 85-101.

DILLARD, Raymond B. & LONGMAN III, Tremper : *An Introduction to the Old Testament*, Grand Rapids, Zondervan, 1994, p. 391-393.

DONOVAN TURNER, Mary : "Jonah 3:10-4:11" in *Interpretation* 52 (1998) p. 411-414.

DYCK, Elmer : "Jonah among the Prophets : A Study in Canonical Context" in *Journal of the Evangelical Theological Society* 33/1 (1990) p. 63-73.

ELLISON, H. L. : *Jonah* (The Expositor's Bible Commentary, vol. 7, ed. F. E. Gaebelein), Grand Rapids, Zondervan, 1985, p. 361-391.

ELLUL, J. : *Le livre de Jonas,* Cahors, Coueslant, 1952, 104 p.

ERMONI, V. : "Jonas" in *Dictionnaire de la Bible,* Vol. 3.2, pub. Vigouroux, Paris, Letouzey, 1926, col. 1604-1613.

EXELL, Joseph S. : *Jonah* (The Biblical Illustrator), London, Griffiths, 1905, 81 p.

FEINBERG, Charles L. : *The Minor Prophets*, Chicago, Moody, 1951, p. 133-152.

FERGUSON Paul : "Who was the 'King of Nineveh' in Jonah 3.6 ?" in *Tyndale Bulletin* 47.2 (1996) p. 301-314.

FEUILLET, A. : "Jonas (le livre de)" in *Supplément au dictionnaire de la Bible,* Vol. 4, dir. Pirot, Paris, Letouzey, 1979, col. 1104-1131.

FRANCE, R. T. : *Jesus and the Old Testament : his Application of Old Testament Passages to himself and his Mission*, London, Tyndale, 1971, p. 43-46, 53-55.

FREEMAN, Hobart E. : *An Introduction to the Old Testament Prophets*, Chicago, Moody, 1968, p. 160-171.

FRETHEIM, Terence E. : "Jonah and Theodicy" in *Zeitschrift für alttestamentliche Wissenschaft* (1978) p. 227-237.

FROLOV, Serge : "Returning the Ticket : God and his Prophet in the Book of Jonah" in *Journal for the Study of the Old Testament* 86 (1999) p. 85-105.

GAEBELEIN, Frank E. : *Four Minor Prophets,* Chicago, Moody, 1970, p. 55-138.

GODET, Frédéric, dir. : "Jonas" in *Bible annotée*, vol. 9. Rééd. St-Légier, Emmaüs, 1981, p. 115-130

GUERS, E. : *Jonas fils d'Amitthaï ou méditations sur la mission de ce prophète*, Genève, Beroud et Guers, 1847, 370 p.

GUILLAUME, Philippe : "Jonas 4" in *Lire et Dire* 35 (1998) p. 17-27.

HALPERN, Baruch ; FRIEDMAN, Richard Elliott : "Composition and Paronomasia in the Book of Jonah" in *Hebrew Annual Review* 4 (1980) p. 79-92.

HARRISON, Roland Kenneth : *Introduction to the Old Testament,* Grand Rapids, Eerdmans, 1969, p. 904-918.

HAUSER, Alan Jon : "Jonah : in Pursuit of the Dove" in *Journal of Biblical Literature* 104/1 (1985) p. 21-37.

HÖFFKEN, Peter : "Das Ende des Jonabuches. Eine Anmerkung zu Jona 4,11" in *Theologische Zeitschrift* 56 (2000) p. 289-297.

HOLBERT, John C. : "'Deliverance belongs to Yahweh' : Satire in the Book of Jonah" in *Journal for the Study of the Old Testament* 21 (1981) p. 59-81.

JENSEN, Irving L. : *Minor Prophets of Israel*, Chicago, Moody, 1975, p. 18-42.

JOSÈPHE, Flavius : *Antiquities of the Jews* IX.XI (ou IX.X.1-2).

KEDDIE, Gordon : *Prophète en fuite,* Chalon-sur-Saône, Europresse, 1990, 142 p.

KEIL, C. F. : *Minor Prophets* (Commentary on the Old Testament, vol. 10, ed. Keil & Delitzsch), Grand Rapids, Eerdmans, s.d., p. 379-417.

KIDNER, F. Derek : "The Distribution of Divine Names in Jonah" in *Tyndale Bulletin* 21 (1970) p. 126-128.

KOHLENBERGER III, John R. : *Jonah and Nahum* (Everyman's Bible Commentary), Chicago, Moody, 1984, p. 15-75.

KUEN, Alfred : *Encyclopédie des difficultés bibliques : Évangiles et Actes*, St-Légier, Emmaüs, 2002, 771 p.

LACOCQUE, A. & P.-E. : *Le complexe de Jonas. Une étude psycho-religieuse du prophète*, Paris, Cerf, 1989, 320 p.

LANDES, George M. : "Textual 'Information Gaps' and 'Dissonances' in the Interpretation of the Book of Jonah" in *Ki Baruch Hu. Ancient Near Eastern, Biblical, and Judaic Studies in Honor of Baruch A. Levine*, ed. R.Chazan, Winona Lake, Eisenbrauns, 1999, p. 273-293.

LAWRENCE, Paul J.N. : "Assyrian nobles and the book of Jonah" in *Tyndale Bulletin* 37 (1986) p. 121-132.

LAWSON, Steven J. : "The Power of Biblical Preaching : An Expository Study of Jonah 3:1-10" in *Bibliotheca Sacra* 158 (2001) p. 331-346.

LEGRAND, Thierry : "Jonas 3: 'Qui sait...'" in *Lire et Dire* 38 (1998), p. 17-26.

LEVINE, Etan : "Jonah as a Philosophical Book" in *Zeitschrift für alttestamentliche Wissenschaft* (1984) p. 235-245.

------- "Reopening the Case of Jonah vs. God" in *Heaven and Earth, Law and Love. Studies in Biblical Thought*, ed. E.Levine (Beihefte zur Zeitschrift für die alttestamentliche Wissenschaft 303), Berlin, de Gruyter, 2000, p. 67-96.

LICHTERT, Claude : "Par terre et par mer ! Analyse rhétorique de Jonas 1" in *Ephemerides theologicae Lovanienses* 78 (2002) p. 5-24

MARTIN, Hugh : *The Prophet Jonah*, London, Banner of Truth Trust, 1870, 359 p.

MAIER, Gerhard : *Der Prophet Jona* (Wuppertaler Studienbibel), Wuppertal, Brockhaus, 1976, 109 p.

MERRILL, Eugene H. : "The sign of Jonah" in *Journal of the Evangelical Theological Society*, 1980, p. 23-30.

MILES, John R. : "Laughing at the Bible : Jonah as Parody" in *On Humour and the Comic in the Hebrew Bible*, ed. Y.Radday (Journal for the Study of the Old Testament. Supplement Series 92), Sheffield, Almond Press, 1990, p. 202-215.

MORA, Vincent : "Jonas, un conte théologique" in *Monde de la Bible* 84 (1993) p. 38.

NORTH, Robert : *Exégèse pratique des petits prophètes postexiliens*, Rome, Biblico, 1969, p. 128-143.

ORTH, Michael : "Genre in Jonah : The Effects of Parody in the Book of Jonah" in *The Bible in the Light of Cuneiform Literature. Scripture in Context III,* ed. W.Hallo (Ancient Near Eastern Texts and Studies 8), Lewiston, The Edwin Mellen Press, 1990, p. 257-281.

OVERDUIN : Jan : *The Adventures of a Deserter : A Modern Parable from an Ancient Story*, Exeter, Paternoster, 1965, 152 p.

PARROT, André : *Ninive et l'Ancien Testament* (Cahiers d'archéologie biblique 3), Neuchâtel, Delachaux et Niestlé, 190, 80 p.

PAYNE, David F. : "Jonah from the Perspective of its Audience" in *Journal for the Study of the Old Testament* 13 (1979) p. 3-12.

PERSON, Raymond F. Jr. : *Conversation with Jonah. Conversation Analysis, Literary Criticism, and the Book of Jonah* (Journal for the Study of the Old Testament. Supplement Series 220, 1996), Sheffield, Sheffield Academic Press, 204 p.

PREISWERK, M. : "Jonas" in *Explication des douze derniers livres prophétiques*, Neuchâtel, Michaud, 1841, p. 3-21.

PRITCHARD, James B. : *Ancient Near Eastern Texts relating to the Old Testament,* Princeton, Princeton University, 1969, 490 p.

PRICE, Brynmor F. & NIDA, Eugene A. : *A Translators Handbook on the Book of Jonah*, Stuttgart, United Bible Societies, 1978, 95 p.

------- "The Book of Jonah" in *A Handbook on the Books of Obadiah, Jonah, and Micah*, New York, United Bible Societies, 1993, p. 44-115.

RATNER, Robert J. : "Jonah, the Runaway Servant" in *Sopher Mahir. Northwest Semitic Studies Presented to Stanislav Segert*, ed. E.Cook, Winona Lake, Eisenbrauns, 1990, p. 281-305.

REICHELBERG, Ruth : *L'aventure prophétique. Jonas, menteur de Vérité*, Paris, Albin Michel, 1995, 262 p.

ROBINSON, Bernard P. : "Jonah's Qiqayon Plant" in *Zeitschrift für alttestamentliche Wissenschaft* (1985) p. 390-403.

ROBINSON, D. W. B. : "Jonas" in *Nouveau Commentaire Biblique*, dir. Guthrie et al., St-Légier, Emmaüs, 1978, p. 780-785.

ROLDANUS, Johannes : "Usages variés de Jonas par les premiers Pères" in *Figures de l'Ancien Testament chez les Pères* (Cahiers de Biblia Patristica 2), 1989, p. 159-188.

SCHERMAN, Nosson & ZLOTOWITZ, Meir : *Jonas : traduction et commentaires fondés sur les sources talmudiques, midrachiques et rabbiniques*, Paris, Colbo, 1990, 154 p.

SCHRADER, Stephen R. : "Jonah" in *Evangelical Commentary on the Bible*, ed. Walter A. Elwell, Grand Rapids, Baker, 1989, p. 644-649.

SHERWOOD, Yvonne : "Rocking the Boat : Jonah and the New Historicism" in *Biblical Interpretation* 5 (1997) p. 364-402.

------- "Cross-Currents in the Books of Jonah : Some Jewish and Cultural Midrashim on a Traditional Text" in *Biblical Interpretation* 6 (1998) p. 49-79.

SMELIK, K.A.D. : "The Literary Function of Poetical Passages in Biblical Narrative. The Case of Jonah 2:3-10" in *Give Ear to my Words. Psalms and other Poetry in and around the Hebrew Bible. Essays in honour of Professor N. A. van Uchelen*, ed. J.Dyk, Amsterdam, Societas Hebraica Amstelodamensis, 1996, p. 147-151.

SPANGENBERG, I.J.J. : "Jonah and Qohelet : Satire Versus Irony" in *Old Testament Essays* 9 (1996) p. 495-511.

SWETNAM, James : "Some Signs of Jonah" in *Biblica* 68 (1987) p. 74-79.

TATFORD, Fredk. A. : *Prophet who deserted : An Exposition of the Book of Jonah*, Eastbourne (GB), Prophetic Witness, 1974, 88 p.

THOUVENOT, Ed. : *Le prophète Jonas*, Genève, Robert, 1911, 73 p.

TRIBLE, Phyllis : "A Tempest in a Text : Ecological Soundings in the Book of Jonah" in *Theology Digest* 43, 1996, 303-312.

------- "Divine Incongruities in the Book of Jonah" in *God in the Fray. A Tribute to Walter Brueggemann*, ed. T.Linafelt, Minneapolis, Fortress Press, 1998, p. 198-208.

VILLEY, Lucile : "La lecture des Pères" *Cahiers Évangile. Supplément* 110 (2000) p. 49-79.

WALTON, John & BEYER, Bryan : *Obadiah, Jona* (Bible Study Commentary), Grand Rapids, Zondervan, 1982, p. 11-81.

WEISS, G. Christian : *Wrong-way Jonah*, Reading (GB), Back to the Bible Broadcast, 1967, 126 p.

WENDLAND, Ernst, R. : "Text Analysis and the Genre of Jonah (part 2)" in *Journal of the Evangelical Theological Society* 39/3 (1996) p. 373-395.

WILLIAMS, W. C. : "Jonah, Book of" in *The International Standard Bible Encyclopedia*, vol. 2, ed. Bromiley, Grand Rapids, Eerdmans, 1982, p. 1112-1116.

WILLIS, John T. : "The 'Repentance' of God in the Books of Samuel, Jeremiah, and Jonah" in *Horizons in Biblical Theology* 16 (1994) p. 156-175.

WILSON, Ambrose John : "The Sign of the Prophet Jonah and its Modern Confirmations" in *Princeton Theological Review* 25 (1927) p. 630-642.

WISEMAN, Donald J. : "Jonah's Nineveh" in *Tyndale Bulletin* 30 (1979) p. 29-51.

WOLFF, Hans Walter[1] : *Obadiah and Jonah*, Minneapolis, Augsburg Pub., 1986, p. 75-177.

WOOD, Leon J. : *The Prophets of Israel*, Grand Rapids, Baker, 1979, p. 289-294.

1 This author provides an important bibliography on Jonah.

Books by the same author published in French by
Editions Emmaüs route de Fenil 40, CH-1806 Saint-Légier
http://www.institut-emmaus.ch/editions/presentation.html

Bible Commentaries

- Le livre des Juges. Ces mystérieux héros de la foi. (395 pages)
- Ruth à la croisée des chemins (135 pages)
- Elie entre le jugement et la grâce. Commentaire de 1 Rois 17 à 2 Rois 2 (195 pages)
- Elisée, précurseur de Jésus-Christ. Commentaire de 2 Rois 2-9 (215 pages).
- Esther: survivre dans un monde hostile (199 pages)
- L'évangile de Marc: puissance et souffrance de Jésus-Christ (503 pages)

Reference work on Ethics

- Vivre l'éthique de Dieu. L'amour et la justice au quotidien. (400 pages)

Collection of plays

- Théâtre pour Noël, volume 1 (140 pages)
- Théâtre pour Noël, volume 2 (217 pages)

CPSIA information can be obtained at www.ICGtesting.com
Printed in the USA
LVOW11s1727140715

446202LV00002B/408/P

9 781502 764140